Social Media Marketing

FOR

DUMMIES®

POCKET EDITION

**by Jan Zimmerman
and
Doug Sahlin**

WILEY

John Wiley & Sons, Inc.

Social Media Marketing For Dummies®, Pocket Edition

Published by
John Wiley & Sons, Inc.
111 River Street
Hoboken, NJ 07030-5774

www.wiley.com

Copyright © 2011 by John Wiley & Sons, Inc., Hoboken, New Jersey

Published by John Wiley & Sons, Inc., Hoboken, New Jersey

Published simultaneously in Canada

For general information on our other products and services, please contact our
Customer Care Department within the U.S. at 877-762-2974, outside the U.S. at 317-572-
3993, or fax 317-572-4002.

For technical support, please visit www.wiley.com/techsupport.

Wiley also publishes its books in a variety of electronic formats. Some content that
appears in print may not be available in electronic books.

ISBN: 978-1-118-17799-0

Manufactured in the United States of America

10 9 8 7 6 5 4 3 2 1

WILEY

Publisher's Acknowledgments

We're proud of this book; please send us your comments at http://dummies.
custhelp.com. For other comments, please contact our Customer Care Department
within the U.S. at 877-762-2974, outside the U.S. at 317-572-3993, or fax 317-572-4002.
Some of the people who helped bring this book to market include the following:

*Acquisitions, Editorial, and
Media Development*

Project Editor: Rebecca Senninger

Acquisitions Editor: Amy Fandrei

Copy Editor: Rebecca Whitney

Technical Editor: Michelle Oxman

Editorial Manager: Kevin Kirschner

Media Development Project Manager:
Laura Moss-Hollister

**Media Development Assistant Project
Manager:** Jenny Swisher

Editorial Assistant: Amanda Graham

Sr. Editorial Assistant: Cherie Case

Cartoons: Rich Tennant
(www.the5thwave.com)

Composition Services

Project Coordinator: Kristie Rees

Layout and Graphics: Claudia Bell,
Carl Byers, Lavonne Roberts

Proofreaders: Laura Bowman,
Susan Moritz

Publishing and Editorial for Technology Dummies

    Richard Swadley, Vice President and Executive Group Publisher

    Andy Cummings, Vice President and Publisher

    Mary Bednarek, Executive Acquisitions Director

    Mary C. Corder, Editorial Director

Publishing for Consumer Dummies

    Kathleen Nebenhaus, Vice President and Executive Publisher

Composition Services

    Debbie Stailey, Director of Composition Services

Table of Contents

. . . .

Introduction

● ●

*Y*ou sit back, sighing with relief that your website is running faultlessly, optimized for search engines, and producing traffic, leads, and sales. Maybe you've ventured into e-mail marketing or pay-per-click advertising to generate new customers. Now, you think with satisfaction, "I'll just let the money roll in."

Instead, you're inundated with stories about Facebook and fan pages, Twitter and tweets, blogs and vlogs, and all other manner of social media buzz. The statistics are astounding: Facebook has over 750 million active users; 150 million blogs are on the Internet; billions of tweets have been sent on Twitter since 2006; more than 2 billion videos are streamed daily on YouTube. New company names and bewildering new vocabulary terms flood the online world: Gowalla, Groupon, SocialMention, CoTweet, engagement, community building, content posting, and comment monitoring, for example.

Should your business get involved in social media marketing? Is it all more trouble than it's worth? Will you be left hopelessly behind if you don't participate? If you jump in, how do you keep it all under control and who does the work? This book helps you answer both sets of questions: Should or shouldn't your business undertake social media marketing? If so, how? (Quick answer: If your customers use a social media service, you should consider it. If not, skip it.)

About This Book

Social Media Marketing For Dummies, Pocket Edition is divided into five parts:

Part I explains what social media services are, categorizes the overwhelming number of social media options by type, and explores how social media are the same and different from other forms of marketing.

Part II helps you decide which forms of social media fit your target market so that you can develop a marketing strategy.

Part III shows you how to manage your social media schedule and campaign. We cover legal issues here, as well.

Part IV explains how to gain invaluable market intelligence and how to keep your audience engaged.

Part V offers a variety of productivity tools to help you post content in multiple locations, notify search engines, and monitor your growing social notoriety.

Icons Used in This Book

To make your experience easier, we use various icons in the margins to identify special categories of information.

These hints help you save time, energy, or aggravation. Sharing them is our way of sharing what we've figured out the hard way — so that you don't have to. Of course, if you prefer to get your education through the school of hard knocks, be our guest.

This icon reminds you of points made elsewhere in the book or perhaps helps you recall business best practices that you know from your own experience.

Heed these warnings to avoid potential pitfalls. We tell you about business and legal pitfalls to avoid, plus a few traps that catch the unprepared during the process of configuring social media services.

The geeky-looking Dummies Man marks information to share with your developer or programmer — unless you are one. In that case, have at it. On the other hand, you can skip any of the technical-oriented information without damaging your marketing plans or harming a living being.

Where to Go from Here

You can find helpful information on the companion website for this book at www.dummies.com/go/socialmediamarketingaio. From the site, you can download copies of the Social Media Goals and Social Media Marketing Plan forms, which you can use to develop your own marketing plans. You can also find an online Cheat Sheet to print and keep handy near your computer at www.dummies.com/cheatsheet/socialmediamarketingaio.

If you find errors in this book, or have suggestions for future editions, please e-mail us at books@watermelonweb.com. We wish you a fun and profitable experience going social!

Part I

Making the Business Case for Social Media

*I*n the best of all worlds, social media — a suite of online services that facilitates two-way communication and content sharing — can become a productive component of your overall marketing strategy. These services can enhance your company's online visibility, strengthen relationships with your clients, and expand word-of-mouth advertising, which is the best type.

Given its rapid rise in popularity and its hundreds of millions of worldwide users, social media marketing sounds quite tempting. These tools require minimal upfront cash, and, theoretically, you'll find customers flooding through your cyberdoors, ready to buy. It sounds like a no-brainer — but it isn't.

Has someone finally invented a perfect marketing method that puts you directly in touch with your customers and prospects, costs nothing, and generates profits faster than a perpetual motion machine produces energy? The hype is yes; the real answer, unfortunately, is no. Marketing nirvana is not yet at hand.

This part provides an overview of the pros and cons of social media to help you decide whether to join the social whirl and gives a framework for approaching a strategic choice of which media to use.

Making Your Social Debut

Like any form of marketing, social media takes some thought. It can become an enormous siphon of your time, and short-term profits are rare. Social media is a long-term marketing commitment.

So, should you or shouldn't you invest time and effort in this new marketing avenue? If you answer in the affirmative, you immediately confront another decision: What form should that investment take? The number of options is overwhelming; you can never use every technique and you certainly can't do them all at once.

Figure 1-1 shows how small businesses are using social media. According to a 2011 survey from social marketing company Constant Contact, nearly 75 percent of small-business owners are using social media to promote their business. The survey showed that of those businesses that are not currently using social media marketing, 62 percent expect to begin doing so within the next 12 months.

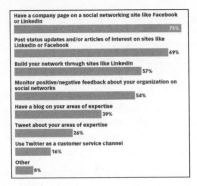

Courtesy eMarketer

Figure 1-1: Of the 75 percent of small businesses using social media, the greatest number created profile pages on social networking sites as part of their strategy.

Defining Social Media Marketing

The bewildering array of social media (which seem to breed new services faster than rabbits) makes it hard to discern what they have in common: shared information, often on a peer-to-peer basis. Although many social media messages look like traditional "broadcasts" from one business to many consumers, their interactive component offers an enticing illusion of "one-to-one" communication that invites individual readers to respond.

The phrase *social media marketing* generally refers to using these online services for relationship selling — a subject you already know all about. *Social media services* or *channels* make innovative use of new online technologies to accomplish familiar communication and marketing goals.

Everything you already know about marketing is correct. Social media marketing is a new technique, not a new world.

This book covers a variety of *social media services* or *channels*. You may hear social media referred to as *Web 2.0* (interactive) techniques. At least one prominent marketing company distinguishes between the two, constraining the term *Web 2.0* to enabling technologies and reserving *social media* for relationship-building activities.

For the purpose of this book, this distinction is somewhat academic. Instead, we group tools that improve the performance or effectiveness of social media into one category, regardless of the underlying technology. We use the phrase *social media site* to refer to a specific, named online service or product.

You can categorize social media services (or *channels*) into categories. The channels have fuzzy boundaries: They may overlap, and some sites fall into multiple channels. For instance, some social networks and communities allow participants to share photos and may include a blog.

Here are the different types of social media channels:

- ✔ **Blogs:** websites designed to let you easily update or change content and allow readers to post their own opinions or reactions. Figure 1-2 shows you an example of a business blog with verve, from Crafty Chica. Her blog, which is only part of a suite of her social media activities, exchanges messages with Facebook and Twitter.

  Examples of blogging software are

  - WordPress, TypePad, and Blogger (formerly Blogspot) (freestanding blog services)

  - Other blog software, freestanding sites, or blogs integrated into standard websites

Courtesy CraftyChica.com
Figure 1-2: A Diary of a Crafty Chica is a blog on Blogspot.

- **Social networking services:** Originally developed to facilitate the exchange of personal information (messages, photos, video, audio) to groups of friends and family, these full-featured services offer multiple functions. From a business point of view, many of them support subgroups that offer the potential for more targeted marketing.

  - *Full networks* such as Facebook, MySpace, or myYearbook

    Figure 1-3 shows the Facebook site of ArtBizCoach.com, which teaches artists how to promote their art.

  - *Microblogging (short message) networks* such as Twitter or Plurk

    Figure 1-4 shows how ScaniaGroup, a B2B manufacturer of trucks and buses, uses its Twitter account to provide information and alert customers to new opportunities.

- *Professional networks* such as LinkedIn and Plaxo

- *Other specialty networks within vertical industry, demographic, or activity segments*

✔ **Social-media sharing services:** These media channels facilitate posting and commenting on videos, photos, and podcasts (audio):

- *Video:* Examples are YouTube, Vimeo, or Ustream. Figure 1-5 shows how the Roger Smith Hotel takes advantage of its YouTube channel.

- *Photos:* Flickr, Photobucket, or Picasa

- *Audio:* Podcast Alley or BlogTalkRadio

Alyson Stanfield's community page for ArtBiz /Stanfield Art Associates at facebook.com/ artbizcoach

Figure 1-3: Companies use the popular social networking service Facebook to maintain an ongoing public dialogue with colleagues, customers, and prospects.

Figure 1-4: Twitter, a rapidly growing, microblogging social network, is excellent for disseminating announcements, events, sales notices, and promotions and for quickly alerting customers of new information.

✔ **Social bookmarking services:** Similar to private bookmarks for your favorite sites on your computer, social bookmarks are publicly viewable lists of sites that others have recommended:

- *Recommendation services* such as StumbleUpon, Delicious

- *Social shopping services* such as Kaboodle or ThisNext

- *Other bookmarking services organized by topic or application,* such as book recommendation sites

Courtesy Roger Smith Hotel

Figure 1-5: The YouTube channel for the Roger Smith Hotel is an integral part of its social media strategy.

✔ **Social news services:** On these peer-based lists of recommended articles from news sites, blogs, or web pages, users often "vote" on the value of the postings:

- Digg
- reddit
- Other news sites

✔ **Social geolocation and meeting services:** For a change, these services bring people together in real space rather than in cyberspace:

- Foursquare, Gowalla, Loopt
- Other GPS (global positioning system) applications, many of which operate on mobile phones
- Meet-ups and tweet-ups

✔ **Community building services:** Many comment-
and content-sharing sites have been around
for a long time, such as forums, message
boards, and Yahoo! and Google groups. Other
examples are

- *Community building sites* with multiple sharing
  features such as *Ning*

- *Wikis* such as Wikipedia for group-sourced
  content

- *Review sites* such as TripAdvisor and
  Epinions to solicit consumer views

Dozens, if not hundreds, of social tools, apps (freestanding online applications), and widgets (small
applications placed on other sites, services, or desk-
tops) monitor, distribute, search, analyze, and rank
content. Many are specific to a particular social network, especially Twitter.

Others are designed to aggregate information across
the social media landscape, including such monitoring tools as Google Alerts or Social Mention or distribution tools such as RSS or Ping.fm.

Understanding the Benefits of Social Media

Social media marketing carries many benefits. One of
the most important is that you don't have to front any
cash for most services. Of course, there's a downside:
Most services require a significant investment of time
to initiate and maintain a social media marketing
campaign.

As you read the list of benefits, think about whether
the benefit is one that applies to your needs. How

important is it to your business? How much time are you willing to allocate to it? What kind of a payoff would you expect? Figure 1-6 shows how small businesses rate the relative effectiveness of social media in meeting their goals.

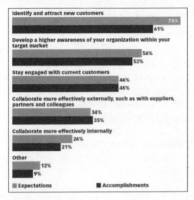

Identify and attract new customers
73%
61%

Develop a higher awareness of your organization within your target market
56%
52%

Stay engaged with current customers
46%
46%

Collaborate more effectively externally, such as with suppliers, partners and colleagues
34%
35%

Collaborate more effectively internally
26%
21%

Other
12%
9%

■ Expectations   ■ Accomplishments

Courtesy eMarketer
Figure 1-6: eMarketer surveyed how small businesses rate the effectiveness of social media in meeting their goals.

Casting a wide net to catch your target market

The audience for social media is huge. In July 2011, Facebook claimed more than 750 million users, many of whom use the service multiple times per week (and others who never use it after the first time). By mid-March 2010, weekly traffic on Facebook had exceeded weekly traffic on Google, which had worn the traffic crown for years. Twitter claims more than 175 million users and insists that millions of *tweets* (short messages) are posted daily. Even narrowly focused networking sites claim hundreds of thousands of visitors.

A relatively small number of power users — those who post ten or more times per day — drive a huge number of tweets. The vast majority of users either read messages only, without posting, or post only one or two messages per week. It's probably the old 80/20 rule at play: 80 percent of the users produce 20 percent of the tweets, and 20 percent of the users produce 80 percent of the tweets!

Surely, some of the people using these sites must be your customers or prospects. In fact, one popular use of social media is to cast a wide net to capture more potential visitors to your website. The classic conversion funnel shown in Figure 1-7 shows the value of bringing new traffic to the top of the funnel.

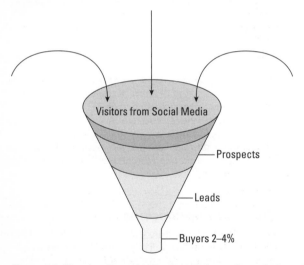

Figure 1-7: The classic conversion funnel shows that only 2 to 4 percent of funnel entries yield desired results.

If more people arrive at the top of the funnel, theoretically more will progress through the steps of prospect and qualified lead to become a customer. Only 2 to 4 percent, on average, make it through a funnel regardless of what the funnel decision is.

 In Part II, we discuss how you can assess traffic on social media sites using tools such as Quantcast or Alexa and match their visitors to the profiles of your customers.

Branding

Basic marketing focuses on the need for branding, name recognition, visibility, presence, or top-of-mind awareness. Call it what you will — you want people to remember your company name when they're in need of your product or service. Social media services, of almost every type, are excellent ways to build your brand.

 Social media works for branding as long as you get your name in front of the right people. Plan to segment the audience on the large social media services. You can look for more targeted groups within them or search for specialty services that may reach fewer people overall but more of the ones who are right for your business.

Building relationships

You will hear repeatedly that social media marketing requires the long view. To build effective relationships in social media, you're expected to

✔ Establish your expertise.

✔ Participate regularly as a "good citizen" of whichever social media world you're inhabiting.

> ✔ Avoid overt self-promotion.
>
> ✔ Sell softly.
>
> ✔ Provide value with links, resources, and unbiased information.

Watch for steady growth in the number of your followers on a particular service; the number of people who recommend your site to others; increased downloads of white papers; or repeat visits to your site. All these signs indicate you're building relationships that may later lead, if not to a direct sale, then to a word-of-Web recommendation to someone who does buy.

In the world of social media, the term *engagement* refers to the length of time and quality of interaction between your company and your followers.

 Social media is a long-term commitment. Other than little experiments or pilot projects, don't bother starting a social media commitment if you don't plan to keep it going. Any short-term benefits you see aren't worth the effort you have to make.

Improving business processes

Already, many clever businesses have found ways to use social media to improve business processes. Though individual applications depend on the nature of your business, consider leveraging social media to

> ✔ Promptly detect and correct customer problems or complaints.
>
> ✔ Obtain customer feedback and input on new product designs or changes.
>
> ✔ Provide tech support to many people at one time; if one person has a question, changes are good that others do, too.

- ✔ Improve service delivery, such as cafés that accept to-go orders on Twitter or Facebook or cupcake carts and food caravans that notify customers where and when their carts will arrive.

- ✔ Locate qualified new vendors, service providers, and employees by using professional networks such as LinkedIn.

- ✔ Collect critical market intelligence on your industry and competitors by watching content on appropriate social media.

- ✔ Use new geolocation services to drive local traffic during slow times and acquire new customers.

 Marketing is only part of your company, but all of your company is marketing. Social media is a ripe environment for this hypothesis, where every part of a company, from human resources to tech support, and from engineering to sales, can be involved.

Improving search engine rankings

Just as you optimize your website, you should optimize your social media outlets for search engine ranking. Now that search engines are cataloging Twitter and Facebook and other appearances on social media, you can gain additional front page real estate for your company on Google, Yahoo!, and Bing.

Search engines recognize some, but not all, appearances on social media as inbound links, which also improve the page rank of your site.

 Use a core set of search terms and keywords across as many sites as possible.

Optimization pays off in other ways: in results on real-time searches, which are now available on primary search engines; on external search engines that focus on blogs or other social media services; and on internal, site-specific search engines.

Selling when opportunity arises

Conventional thinking says that social media is designed for long-term engagement, for marketing and branding rather than for sales. However, a few obvious selling opportunities exist, particularly for business-to-consumer (B2C) companies, that won't offend followers:

- ✔ **Sell CDs and event tickets.** Services such as MySpace cater to music and entertainment and are considered appropriate places.

- ✔ **Include a link to your store on social shopping services.** Recommend products — particularly apparel, jewelry, beauty, and decor — as Stylehive does.

- ✔ **Offer promotional codes or special offers to followers.** Offering them on particular networks encourages your followers to visit your site to make a purchase. You can even announce sales or events.

- ✔ **Place links to online or third-party stores on your profile pages on various services.** You can rarely sell directly from a social media service, but some permit you to place widgets that visually showcase your products and link to your online store, PayPal, or the equivalent to conclude a transaction.

- ✔ **Include a sign-up option for your e-newsletter.** It offers a bridge to sales.

The chart in Figure 1-8 shows a 2010 HubSpot survey of the percentage of companies that succeeded in acquiring a customer by way of a specific social media channel. The survey encompassed both B2B companies (on the left of each pairing) and B2C companies (on the right). It shows that many businesses that make the effort succeed in closing sales that were initiated in a social media channel.

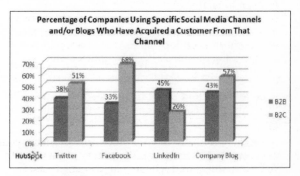

Courtesy HubSpot® www.hubspot.com

Figure 1-8: This survey indicates that you can, with a little effort, make a sale by way of social media.

 Include sales offers within a stream of information and news to avoid turning your social media site into a series of never-ending advertisements. Throughout this book, you read about other businesses that have found unique ways to sell socially.

Saving money on advertising

The magic word is *free*. If you're a start-up company, "free" social media is likely the only advertising you can afford. If you decide to approach social media for this purpose, construct your master campaign just as carefully as you would a paid one:

- ✔ Create a plan that outlines target markets, ad offers, publishing venues, and scheduled "flights" for different ad campaigns.

- ✔ If necessary, conduct comparative testing of messages, graphics, and offers.

- ✔ Monitor results and focus on the outlets that work best at driving qualified visits that lead to conversions.

- ✔ Supplement your free advertising with search optimization and press releases and other forms of free promotion.

Advertising is only one part of marketing!

As you see traffic and conversions building from your social media marketing campaigns, you may want to reduce existing paid advertising campaigns. Just don't stop your paid advertising until you're confident that you have an equally profitable stream of customers from social media. Of course, if your ad campaign isn't working, there's no point continuing it.

Understanding the Cons of Social Media

For all its upsides, social media has its downsides. As social media has gained in popularity, it has also become increasingly difficult to gain visibility among its hundreds of millions of users.

In fact, sometimes you have to craft a campaign just to build an audience on a particular social media site. It's quite similar to conducting optimization and inbound link campaigns so that your site is found in natural search results.

 Don't participate in social media for its own sake, or just because "everyone else is."

By far, the biggest downside in social media is the amount of time you need to invest to see results. You need to make an ongoing commitment to review and respond to comments and to provide an ongoing stream of new material. An initial commitment to set up a profile is just the tip of the iceberg.

If you became addicted to news alerts during the 2008 presidential campaign or couldn't take your eyes off live coverage of the Mars landing, or if you play Farmville or other video games with a passion, continuously run instant messaging, or check e-mail every ten seconds, watch out for social media.

Individually and collectively, social media is the biggest-ever time sink. Without self-discipline and a strong time schedule, you can easily become so socially overbooked that other tasks go undone.

As you consider each of the social media options in this book, consider the level of human resources that are needed. Do you have the time and talents yourself? If not, do other people within your organization have the time and talent? Which other efforts will you need to give up to make room for social media? Will you have to hire new employees or contract out services, leading to hard costs for this supposedly "free" media?

Integrating Social Media into Your Overall Marketing Effort

Social media is only part of online marketing. Online marketing is only part of overall marketing. Don't mistake the part for the whole.

Consider each foray into social marketing as a strategic choice to supplement your other online marketing activities, which may include creating or managing a marketing-effective website, content updates, search engine optimization (SEO), inbound link campaigns, online press releases, event calendar postings, e-mail newsletters, testimonials and reviews, affiliate or loyalty programs, online events or promotions, not to mention pay-per-click ads, banners, or sponsorships.

Social media is neither necessary nor sufficient for all your online marketing.

Use social media strategically to

- ✔ Meet an otherwise unmet marketing need.
- ✔ Increase access to your target market.
- ✔ Open the door to a new niche market.
- ✔ Move prospects through the conversion funnel.
- ✔ Improve the experience for existing customers.

For example, Emerson Salon (http://emerson salon.com; see Figure 1-9) developed a social media presence to attract a younger clientele already actively involved in social networking. For more information on overall online marketing, see Jan's book *Web Marketing For Dummies,* 2nd Edition.

Courtesy Emerson Salon

Figure 1-9: The Emerson Salon maintains an active presence on Facebook, Yelp, and Twitter and has multiple RSS feeds.

You must have a hub site to which Web traffic will be directed, as shown in Figure 1-10. It can be a full-bore website or a blog, as long as the site has its own domain name. It doesn't matter where the site is hosted — only that you own its name, which appears as yourcompany.com or blog.yourcompany.com. Though you can link to yourcompany.wordpress.com, you cannot effectively optimize or search for it. Besides, it doesn't look professional.

Consider sketching for your own campaign a block diagram that shows the relationship between components, the flow of content between outlets, and perhaps even the criterion for success and how it will be measured.

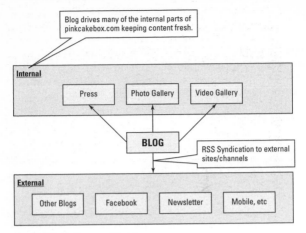

Courtesy Pink Cake Box www.pinkcakebox.com

Figure 1-10: Pink Cake Box developed a block diagram with its blog as its hub, connecting to both internal and external "spokes."

Developing a Strategic Social Media Marketing Plan

Surely you wrote an overall marketing plan when you last updated your business plan and an online marketing plan when you first created your website. If not, it's never too late! For business planning resources, see the Small Business Planner page at www.sba.gov/smallbusinessplanner/plan/writeabusinessplan/index.html or read *Business Plans For Dummies,* 2nd Edition, by Paul Tiffany and Steven D. Peterson.

You can further refine a marketing plan for social media marketing purposes. As with any other marketing plan, you start with a strategy. A Social Media Marketing Strategic goals plan (Figure 1-11 shows an example) would incorporate sections on strategic goals, objectives, target markets, methods, costs, and return on investment (ROI). You can find this statement on this book's website (see the Introduction).

Here are some points to keep in mind when putting together your own strategic marketing overview:

✔ The most important function of the form isn't for you to follow it slavishly, but rather to force you to consider the various facets of social media marketing before you invest too much effort or money.

✔ The form also helps you communicate decisions to your board of advisors or your boss, in case you need to make the business case for getting involved in social media.

✔ The form provides a coherent framework for explaining to everyone involved in your social media effort — employees, volunteers, or contractors — the task you're trying to accomplish and why.

In the following sections, we talk about the information you should include on your form.

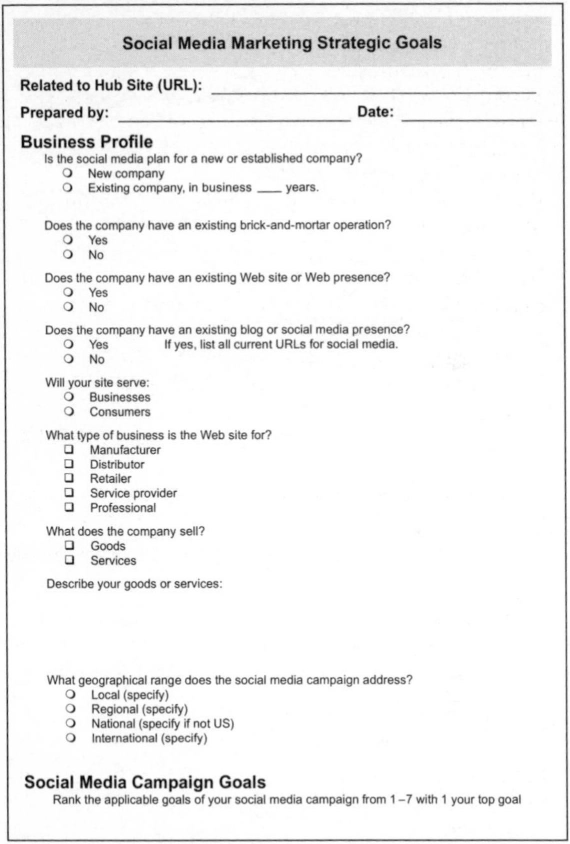

Social Media Marketing Strategic Goals

Related to Hub Site (URL): ____________________

Prepared by: ____________________ **Date:** __________

Business Profile

Is the social media plan for a new or established company?
- ❍ New company
- ❍ Existing company, in business ____ years.

Does the company have an existing brick-and-mortar operation?
- ❍ Yes
- ❍ No

Does the company have an existing Web site or Web presence?
- ❍ Yes
- ❍ No

Does the company have an existing blog or social media presence?
- ❍ Yes If yes, list all current URLs for social media.
- ❍ No

Will your site serve:
- ❍ Businesses
- ❍ Consumers

What type of business is the Web site for?
- ❑ Manufacturer
- ❑ Distributor
- ❑ Retailer
- ❑ Service provider
- ❑ Professional

What does the company sell?
- ❑ Goods
- ❑ Services

Describe your goods or services:

What geographical range does the social media campaign address?
- ❍ Local (specify)
- ❍ Regional (specify)
- ❍ National (specify if not US)
- ❍ International (specify)

Social Media Campaign Goals

Rank the applicable goals of your social media campaign from 1 –7 with 1 your top goal

© 2010 Watermelon Mountain Web Marketing www.watermelonweb.com

Figure 1-11: Establish your own strategic social marketing goals, objectives, and target market definition on this form.

_____ Increasing traffic/visits to hub site

_____ Branding

_____ Building relationships

_____ Improving business process (e.g. customer service, tech support)

_____ Improving visibility in natural search

_____ Increasing sales revenue

_____ Saving money on paid advertising

Financial Profile

Social Media Campaign Budget for First Year

Outside development, contractors, includes writing, design, technical	$ _____
Special content production (e.g. video, podcasts, photography):	$ _____
Marketing/paid ads on social media	$ _____
Inhouse labor (burdened rate)	$ _____
Other costs, e.g. tools, equipment	$ _____
TOTAL:	$ _____

Break-even point: $ _____   Within: _____ mo/yr

Return on investment: % _____   Within: _____ mo/yr

Sample Objectives

Repeat for appropriate objectives for each goal within timeframe specified (for instance, 1 year).

Traffic objective (# visitors per month): _____   Within: _____

Conversion objective: _____ %   Within: _____

Sales objectives (# sales per month): $ _____   Within: _____

Average $ per sale: $ _____   Within: _____

$ revenue per month: $ _____   Within: _____

Other objectives specific to your site, e.g. for branding, relationships, search ranking

_____   Within: _____

_____   Within: _____

_____   Within: _____

Marketing Profile

Describe your target markets. Give specific demographic or other segmentation information. For B2B, segment by industry and/or job title.

_____

_____

_____

_____

_____

_____

_____

What is your marketing tag?

_____

Value proposition: Why should someone buy from your company rather than another?

_____

Name at least six competitors and list their Web sites, blogs, and social media pages

_____   _____

_____   _____

_____   _____

_____   _____

_____   _____

Establishing goals

The Goals section prioritizes the overall reasons you're implementing a social media campaign. You can prioritize your goals from the list of seven benefits of social media, described in the earlier section "Understanding the Benefits of Social Media," or add your own. Most businesses have multiple goals, which you can specify on the form.

Setting quantifiable objectives

For each goal, set at least one quantifiable, measurable objective. "More customers" isn't a quantifiable objective. A quantifiable objective is "Increase number of visits to website by 10 percent," or "add 30 new customers within three months," or "obtain 100 new followers for Twitter account within one month of launch." Enter this information on the form.

Identifying your target markets

Specify one or more target markets on the form, not by what they consume, but rather by who they are. "Everyone who eats dinner out" isn't a submarket you can identify online. However, you can find "high-income couples within 20 miles of your destination who visit wine and classical music sites."

You may want to reach more than one target market by way of social media or other methods. Specify each of them. Then, as you read about different methods in this book, write down next to each one which social media services or sites appear best suited to reach that market. Prioritize the order in which you plan to reach them.

 Think niche!

Estimating costs

Estimating costs from the bottom up is rather tricky, and this approach rarely includes a cap.

Consequently, costs often wildly exceed your budget. Instead, establish first how much money you're willing to invest in the overall effort, including in-house labor, outside contractors, and miscellaneous hard costs such as purchasing software or equipment. Enter those amounts in the Cost section.

Then prioritize your social marketing efforts based on what you can afford, allocating or reallocating funds within your budget as needed. This approach not only keeps your total social marketing costs under control but also lets you assess the results against expenses.

 To make cost-tracking easier, ask your book-keeper or CPA to set up an "activity" or a "job" within your accounting system for social media marketing. Then you can easily track and report all related costs and labor.

Valuing social media ROI

Return on investment (ROI) is your single most important measure of success for social media marketing. In simple terms, *ROI* is the ratio of revenue divided by costs for your business or, in this case, for your social media marketing effort.

You also need to set a realistic term in which you will recover your investment. Are you willing to wait ten weeks? Ten months? Ten years? Some forms of social media are unlikely to produce a fast fix for drooping sales, so consider what you're trying to accomplish.

Figure 1-12 presents a brief glimpse of how others assess the average cost of lead acquisition for B2B companies for social marketing compared to other forms of marketing. It's just a guide. Keep in mind that the only ROI or cost of acquisition that truly matters is your own.

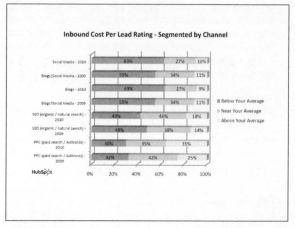

Figure 1-12: This HubSpot chart compares the cost of B2B lead generation for social media and blogs compared to Pay Per Click and natural search.

Costs usually turn out to be simpler to track than revenues that are traceable explicitly to social media.

Whatever you plan online will cost twice as much and take twice as long as anticipated.

Part II

Plotting Your Social Media Marketing Strategy

. . . .

In This Part

▶ Finding your audience online

▶ Segmenting B2C markets

▶ Conducting B2B research online

▶ Planning your strategy

. . . .

*I*n Part I we talk about making the business case for social media marketing, looking at the question of whether you should or shouldn't get involved. This part helps you decide which forms of social media fit your target market. If the previous part was about strategy, goals, and objectives, this one is about tactics.

Let your customers and prospects drive your selection of social media alternatives. To see the best return on your investment in social media, you need to try to use the same social media as they do. This principle is exactly the same one you apply to all your other marketing and advertising efforts. Social media is a new tactic, not a new world.

Fish where your fish are. If your potential customers aren't on a particular social media outlet, don't start a campaign on that media.

In this part, we show how to use online market research to assess the match between your target markets and various social media outlets. After you do that, you're ready to start filling out your own tactical Social Media Marketing Plan, which appears at the end of this part.

Locating Your Target Market Online

Nothing is more important in marketing than identifying and understanding your target audience (or audiences). After you can describe your customers' and prospects' demographic characteristics, where they live and what they do online, you're in a position to focus your social marketing efforts on those people most likely to buy your products or services. (Be sure to include the description of your target market on your Social Media Marketing Strategic Goals plan in Part I.)

Because social media techniques focus on inexpensive ways to reach niche markets with specific messages, they're tailor-made for a guerrilla marketing approach. As with all guerrilla marketing activities, target one market at a time.

Don't dilute your marketing budget or labor by trying to reach too many audiences at a time. People still need to see your message or brand name at least seven times to remember it. Trying to boost yourself to the forefront of everyone's mind all at once is expensive.

Focus your resources on one niche at a time. After you succeed, invest your profits in the next niche. It may seem counterintuitive, but it works.

Don't let setting priorities among niches paralyze you. Your choice of niches usually doesn't matter. If you aren't sure, go for what seems to be the biggest market first, or the easiest one to reach.

Segmenting Your B2C Market

If you have a business-to-consumer company, you can adapt the standard tools of *market segmentation* to define various niche audiences by where they live and how they spend their time and money. The most common types of segmentation are

- ✔ Demographics
- ✔ Geographics
- ✔ Life stages
- ✔ Psychographics or lifestyle
- ✔ Affinity or interest groups

These categories affect not only your social media tactics but also your graphics, message, content, offers, and every other aspect of your marketing strategy.

Your messages need to be specific enough to satisfy the needs and wants of the distinct sub-groups you're trying to reach.

Suppose that you want to sell a line of organic, herbal hair care products using social media. If you described your target market as "everyone who uses shampoo" on your Social Media Marketing Strategic Goals statement (see Part I), segment that market into different subgroups before you select appropriate social marketing techniques.

When you're creating subgroups, keep these concepts in mind:

- ✔ **Simple demographics affect your market definition.** The use of fragrances, descriptive terms, and even packaging may vary by gender. How many shampoo commercials for men talk about silky hair? For that matter, what's the ratio of shampoo commercials addressed to women versus men?

- ✔ **Consider geography.** Geography may not seem obvious, but people who live in dry climates may be more receptive to a message about moisturizers than people who live in humid climates. Or, perhaps your production capacity constrains your initial product launch to a local or regional area.

- ✔ **Think about life stages.** For instance, people who dye their hair look for different hair care products than those who don't, but the reason they color their hair affects your selling message. (Teenagers and young adults may dye their hair unusual colors in an effort to belong to a group of their peers; older men may hide the gray with Grecian Formula; women with kids may be interested in fashion or may color their hair as a pick-me-up.)

- ✔ **Even lifestyles (psychographics) affect decisions.** People with limited resources who are unlikely to try new products may respond to messages about value and satisfaction guarantees; people with more resources or a higher

> status may be affected by messages related to
> social grouping and self-esteem.
>
> ✓ **Affinity or interest groups are an obvious seg-**
> **mentation parameter.** People who participate in
> environmental organizations or who recycle
> goods may be more likely to be swayed by a
> "green shampoo" appeal or shop in specific
> online venues.

Different niche markets are drawn to different social
media activities in general and to specific social
media service providers in particular. In the following
several sections, we look in detail at different online
tools you can use to explore the parameters that
seem the most appropriate for segmenting your audience and selecting specific social media sites.

For more information on market segmentation and
research, see *Small Business Marketing For Dummies,*
by Barbara Findlay Schenck.

 The most successful marketing campaigns are
driven by your target markets, not by
techniques.

Demographics

Demographic segmentation, the most common type
of market differentiation, covers such standard categories as gender, age, ethnicity, marital status, family
size, household income, occupation, social class, and
education.

Sites such as Quantcast (www.quantcast.com) and
Alexa (www.alexa.com) provide basic demographic
information compared to the overall Internet population, as shown in Figure 2-1. Quantcast also displays
the distribution by subcategory within the site. As
you can see, the sites don't always share the same

subcategory breakdowns or completely agree on the data. However, either is close enough for your social marketing purposes.

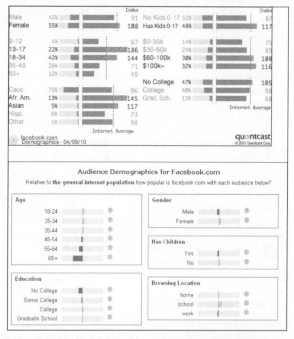

(Top) Courtesy Quantcast.com (Bottom) "Alexa the Web Information Company," "Alexa Top Sites," "Alexa Site Thumbnail," the Alexa® logo and name are trademarks of Amazon.com, Inc. or its affiliates in the United States and/or other countries.

Figure 2-1: Both Quantcast (top) and Alexa (bottom) provide demographic profiles comparing the users of a particular site against the general Internet population.

Use these tools to check out the demographic profile of users on various social media services, as well as your own users and those of your competitors. For instance, we've seen some discussion of MySpace appealing to a more ethnically diverse, younger audience than Facebook does.

Look for a general match between your target audience and that of the social media service you're considering.

Figure 2-2 from Flowtown (www.flowtown.com) shows the correlation between the demographics of Internet users and their use of social media. Of course, these profiles may change over time — sometimes quickly — as a wave of interest washes through a particular demographic segment and then recedes.

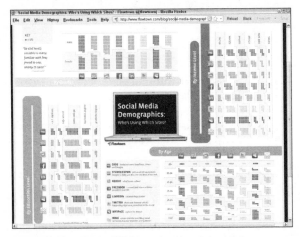

Flowtown: Know your customers? We do.

Figure 2-2: A comparison of demographic profiles (by gender, age, income, and educational level) using eight different social marketing services.

Always check for current information before launching your social media campaign.

Geographics

Marketing by country, region, state, city, zip code, or even neighborhood is obviously the key for location-based social media outlets such as foursquare or Gowalla, mobile marketing with GPS, or any other form of online marketing that involves local search.

Geographic segmentation also makes sense if your business draws its primary target audience from within a certain distance from your brick-and-mortar storefront — for example, grocery stores, barber shops, gas stations, restaurants, movie theaters, and many other service providers, whether or not your social media service itself is location based.

Many social media services offer a location search function to assess the number of users within your geographical target area:

- ✔ **Twitter users within a certain radius:** Enter the city, state, and radius at http://search. twitter.com/advanced.

- ✔ **LinkedIn users within a certain radius:** Enter the zip code or city, state, and radius at www. linkedin.com/search.

- ✔ **Facebook users near a certain location:** Enter a search term, for example, consultants, in the search box and click the magnifying glass icon. Select People in the left navigation. In the Filter By Location box, type a city name, state, region, or zip code. Click the Refine Search button to view results for those people who permit their profiles to appear in search results.

If you can't determine the number of potential users of a service within your specific geo-graphic location, use the Help function, check the blog, or contact the company.

Several companies combine geographical information with demographics and behavioral characteristics to segment the market more finely. For example, the Nielsen Claritas PRIZM, available from Tetrad (www.tetrad.com/demographics/usa/claritas/prizmneappend.html), offers demo-geographic data organized into 66 distinct segments. You can download the list at www.tetrad.com/pub/prices/PRIZMNE_Clusters.pdf.

Again, you're looking for a fit between the profile of your target audience and that of the social media service.

Life stages

Rather than look at a target market solely in terms of demographics, *life stage analysis* considers what people are doing with their lives, recognizing that it may affect media behavior and spending patterns.

Figure 2-3 shows the percentage of Internet users who access social media frequently sorted by life stage.

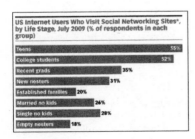

Courtesy eMarketer

Figure 2-3: Recent research indicates that the use of social media varies by stage of life.

With more flexible timing for going through life passages, demographic analysis isn't enough for many types of products and services. Women may have children later in life; many older, non-traditional students go back to college; some retirees re-enter the workforce to supplement social security earnings. What your prospective customers do each day may influence what they buy and which media outlets they use more than their age or location.

Recent research has, in fact, documented that life stages are more likely to predict word-of-mouth and social media behavior than demographics alone. One report found that "new nesters" are the most satisfied (33 percent are very satisfied) with social networking, using it to stay in touch with friends and family. In contrast, the "married, no children cohort," of whom only 20 percent are very satisfied, use social networking primarily to "maintain/expand [their] professional network."

Psychographics or lifestyle

Psychographic segmentation divides a market by social class or lifestyle or by the shared activities, interests, and opinions of prospective customers. It helps identify groups within a social networking service or other, smaller, social networks that attract users meeting your desired profile.

Behavioral segmentation, which is closely related, divides potential buyers based on their uses, responses, or attitudes toward a product or service. To obtain this information about your own customers, consider taking a quick poll as part of your e-newsletter, website, or blog. Although the results from those who reply may not be exactly representative of your total customer base — or that of prospective customers — a survey gives you some starter data.

Don't confuse the psychographic profile of a group with personality traits specific to an individual.

Psychographic segmentation helps you not only identify where to promote your company but also craft your message. For instance, understanding social class might help you determine how to appeal to customers (such as the Innovators or Experiencers shown in Figure 2-4) who might be interested in your high-end line of fashion, home decor, cosmetics, restaurants, or vacation destinations. Or, your ads might show people enjoying a natural, outdoor lifestyle using a product such as organic shampoo.

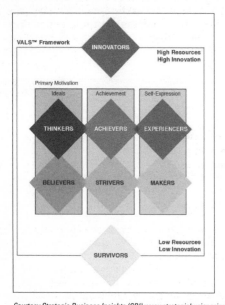

Courtesy Strategic Business Insights (SBI) www.strategicbusinessinsights.com/VALS

Figure 2-4: Psychographic segmentation is shown on the values, attitudes, and lifestyles (VALS) chart.

To develop a better understanding of psychographic profiling, take the quick values, attitudes, and lifestyles (VALS) survey yourself at www.strategicbusinessinsights.com/vals/presurvey.htm.

Affinity, or interest, groups

Segmenting by affinity, or interest, group fills in the blank at the end of the statement "People who like this also like. . . ." Because activity is a subsection of psychographic segmentation, the approach is somewhat similar.

Figure 2-5 shows other interests of Facebook users under the Lifestyle option at the Quantcast site. The Related tab and Clickstream tab at the Alexa site provide lists of other websites that visitors to a particular site also visit.

Courtesy Quantcast.com

Figure 2-5: In this example, Quantcast provides a list of other categories that interest Facebook users.

Using Quantcast and Alexa, you can obtain public information on interest areas for specific social media services or your competitors or other related businesses. You can also use these services to profile your own business, although your website might be too small to provide more than rough estimates. If your business is too small, estimate the interest profile for your target market by running Alexa for a large corporation that offers a similar product or service.

 Request a free profile of your site at www.quantcast.com/user/signup.

Interest categories for your own site, based on the types of other websites your visitors frequent, are also available from a Yahoo! Web Analytics account under Visitor Behavioral Reports (http://web.analytics.yahoo.com/features). Yahoo! Web Analytics free enterprise-level solution is Yahoo's answer to Google Analytics. Otherwise, consider polling your own customers to find out more about their specific interests.

Google Analytics doesn't offer a similar capability, but you can use Google Insights (www.google.com/insights/search/#), which sorts Google searches by interest category, as shown in Table 2-1. Because searches are organized by search term trend, not by source site, you gain a different form of market intelligence.

Table 2-1	Main Categories Available on Google Insights	
Arts and Humanities	Automotive	Beauty and Personal Care
Business	Computers and Electronics	Entertainment

(continued)

Table 2-1 *(continued)*

Finance and Insurance	Food and Drink	Games
Health	Home and Garden	Industries
Internet	Lifestyles	Local
News and Current Events	Photo and Video	Real Estate
Recreation	Reference	Science
Shopping	Social Networks and Online Communities	Society
Sports	Telecommunications	Travel

Researching B2B Markets

Market research and social media choices for business-to-business markets are somewhat different from business-to-consumer markets because the sales cycle is different. Usually, B2B companies have a longer sales cycle, high-ticket purchases, and multiple people who play a role in closing a sale; consequently, B2B marketing requires a different social media presence.

In terms of social media, more B2B marketing efforts focus on branding, top-of-mind visibility, customer support, and problem-solving compared to more sales-focused messages from B2C companies.

You can treat the interest groups in the earlier section "Affinity, or interest, groups" as vertical market segments and take advantage of Google Insights to discern trends over time. You might also want to assess competitor presence on different forms of social media.

One key step in B2B marketing is to identify people who make the buying decision. Professional social networks such as LinkedIn and Plaxo may help you research people on your B2B customer or prospect list.

The value of various forms of social media appears to differ by company size, according to research by Marketing Sherpa, shown in Figure 2-6. Marketing Sherpa also found differences in efficacy by industry type. Their findings may reflect available budget and human resources as well as techniques. For more information, visit www.sherpastore.com/Social MediaMkt2010.html or www.sherpastore.com/B2BMarketingBenchmarkGuide.html to download excerpts. HubSpot, at www.hubspot.com, also offers a range of B2B market research tools and webinars.

As always, the key is ensuring that your customers are using the type of social media you're considering. Use the search feature and group options on major social networking sites to test your list of existing customers. Chances are good that if a large number of your existing customers are using that service, it will be a good source for future customers as well.

In addition to participating in general market research, you might want to try Compete.com, which offers a free basic tool (https://my.compete.com/login/?origin=https://my.compete.com/%3F) that compares as many as five competitors at a time. (More extensive paid versions are also available.) You can use Compete.com to assess audience profiles and export data for your own analysis.

Check competing sites for inbound links from other sites, as well as their own outbound links, to see how they reach their customers.

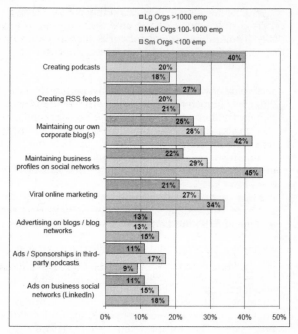

Source: MarketingSherpa.com

Figure 2-6: B2B companies of different sizes find different forms of social media effective for reaching their target audiences.

Conducting Other Types of Market Research Online

The amount of research available online can be paralyzing. A well-crafted search yields most, if not all, of

the social marketing research you need. You aren't
writing an academic paper; you're running a business
with limited time and resources. Set aside a week or
two for research and then start laying out your
approach.

 Don't be afraid to experiment on a small scale.
In the end, what matters is what happens with
your business as you integrate social media into
your marketing plan, not what happens to businesses on the average.

Despite these statements, you might want to touch on
two other research points:

- ✔ **The most influential sites, posters, or pages on
  your preferred social media:** You can learn
  from them.

- ✔ **Understanding what motivates people to use
  certain types of social media:** Make the content
  you provide meet their expectations and
  desires.

Identifying influencers

Whether you have a B2B or B2C company, you gain
valuable insight by seeing which companies or individuals are driving the conversation within your
industry sector. To see the most popular posters
on Twitter, use services such as Klout, at http://
klout.com (by topic), or Twitaholic, at http://
twitaholic.com (by followers or number of posts),
shown in Figure 2-7, to identify people you might want
to follow for research purposes.

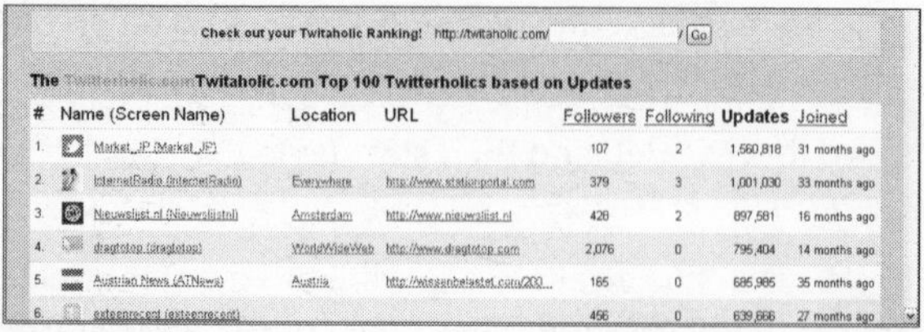
Check out your Twitaholic Ranking! http://twitaholic.com/ / Go

The Twitaholic.com Top 100 Twitterholics based on Updates

#	Name (Screen Name)	Location	URL	Followers	Following	Updates	Joined
1.	Market_JP (Market_JP)			107	2	1,560,818	31 months ago
2.	InternetRadio (InternetRadio)	Everywhere	http://www.stationportal.com	379	3	1,001,030	33 months ago
3.	Nieuwslijst.nl (Nieuwslijstnl)	Amsterdam	http://www.nieuwslijst.nl	428	2	897,581	16 months ago
4.	dragtotop (dragtotop)	WorldWideWeb	http://www.dragtotop.com	2,076	0	795,404	14 months ago
5.	Austrian News (ATNews)	Austria	http://wissenbelastet.com/200...	165	0	685,985	35 months ago
6.	exteenrecent (exteenrecent)			456	0	639,666	27 months ago

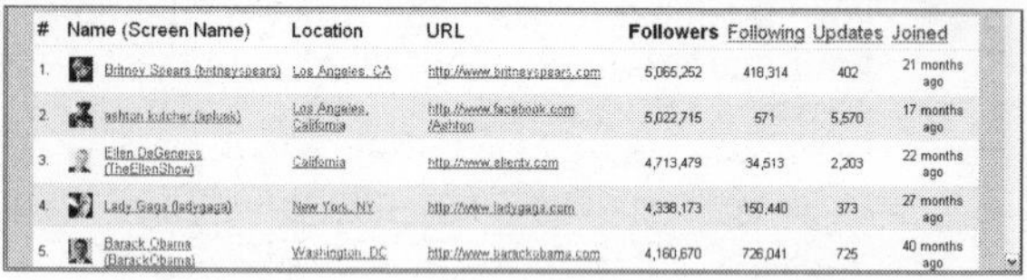

#	Name (Screen Name)	Location	URL	Followers	Following	Updates	Joined
1.	Britney Spears (britneyspears)	Los Angeles, CA	http://www.britneyspears.com	5,065,252	418,314	402	21 months ago
2.	ashton kutcher (aplusk)	Los Angeles, California	http://www.facebook.com/Ashton	5,022,715	571	5,570	17 months ago
3.	Ellen DeGeneres (TheEllenShow)	California	http://www.ellentv.com	4,713,479	34,513	2,203	22 months ago
4.	Lady Gaga (ladygaga)	New York, NY	http://www.ladygaga.com	4,338,173	150,440	373	27 months ago
5.	Barack Obama (BarackObama)	Washington, DC	http://www.barackobama.com	4,160,670	726,041	725	40 months ago

Courtesy Twitaholic.com

Figure 2-7: Twitaholic ranks the most influential tweeters by either number of updates (top) or number of followers (bottom). The most frequent posters aren't the ones with the most followers and vice versa.

Understanding why people use social media services

The expectation that people gravitate toward different types of social media to meet different needs seems reasonable. The challenge, of course, is to match what people seek with particular social sites. The advertising network Chitika compiled the results (`http://chitika.com/research/2010/twitter-and-facebook-are-for-news-myspace-is-for-leisure`) shown in Figure 2-8 by reviewing downstream visits from social networks and sorting them by type. Ask yourself whether these patterns match your expectations and whether they match what you see on these sites.

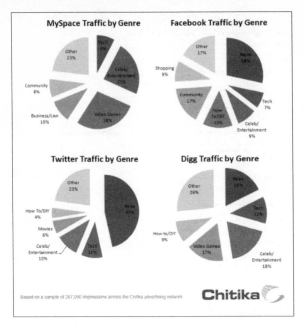

Courtesy Chitika, Inc.

Figure 2-8: Chitika analyzed what users of social media want based on data from its own advertising network.

Setting Up Your Social Marketing Worksheet

You can dive into social media marketing headfirst and see what happens. Or, you can take the time to research, plan, execute, and evaluate your approach. The Social Media Marketing Form, shown in Figure 2-9, is for people taking the latter approach. (You can download the form from this book's website; see the Introduction for more details.)

Social Media Marketing Form
Tactical Options

Company Name _____   Date _____

Hub Site(s)   (URL of Web site or blog with domain name to which traffic will be driven)

_____

Standard Social Media Identification Name/Handle _____

Social Media Project Director _____

Social Media Team Members & Tasks   _____   _____
                                     _____   _____
                                     _____   _____
Programming/Technical Team   _____   _____
Social Media Policy URL   _____

Check boxes for all applications used. Shadow categories are strongly recommended.

SOCIAL MEDIA PLANNING

- ❏   **Dashboard (Select One: Enter URL & Log In Info)**
  - ❏ NetVibes
  - ❏ Hootsuite
  - ❏ Other - Name
  - ❏ Custom
- ❏   **Calendar (Select One: Enter URL & Log In Info)**
  - ❏ Google Calendar
  - ❏ Yahoo! Calendar
  - ❏ Windows Calendar
  - ❏ Other
- ❏   **Social Sharing Service (Select One: Enter URL & Log In Info)**
  - ❏ AddThis
  - ❏ ShareThis
  - ❏ AddToAny
  - ❏ Other
- ❏   **Social Media Resources (Insert One Resource Site or Blog to Follow**
  - ❏

SOCIAL MEDIA TOOL KIT

- ❏   **Monitoring (Select at least one; Enter Name, URL, Log In Info for all used)**
  - ❏ Brand Reputation/Sentiment Tool, e.g. BrandsEye, MyReputation
  - ❏ Topic Monitoring Tool, e.g. Addict-o-Matic, Google Trends
  - ❏ How Sociable
  - ❏ Monitor This
  - ❏ Social Mention
  - ❏ Trackur
  - ❏ WhosTalkin
  - ❏ Blog Monitoring Tool
  - ❏ Twitter Monitoring Tool
  - ❏ Social News, Forums, RSS Monitoring Tool
  - ❏ Google Alerts

Figure 2-9: Build a tactical social media marketing plan for your company.

- ❏ Other
- ❏ **Distribution Tools (Select at least one; Enter Name, URL, & Log In Info for all used)**
  - ❏ RSS/Atom Feeds
  - ❏ ping.fm
  - ❏ Hellotxt
  - ❏ Hootsuite
  - ❏ Only Wire
  - ❏ TweetDeck
  - ❏ Other
- ❏ **Update Notification Tools (Select at least one; Enter Name, URL, Log In Info for all)**
  - ❏ FeedPing
  - ❏ Feed Shark
  - ❏ Google Ping
  - ❏ King Ping
  - ❏ Other
- ❏ **URL Clipping Tool (Select One; Enter URL & Log In Info)**
  - ❏ Bit.ly
  - ❏ SnipURL
  - ❏ TinyURL
  - ❏ Other
- ❏ **Ecommerce Tool or Widget (Select One: Enter URL & Log In Info)**
  - ❏ Netcarnation
  - ❏ CartFly
  - ❏ SELLit
  - ❏ ShopIt
  - ❏ ProductCart
  - ❏ Etsy Widget
  - ❏ Amazon Widget
  - ❏ Paypal Widget
  - ❏ Custom Widget
  - ❏ Other
- ❏ **Search Engine Tools (If needed, enter URL & Log In Info; include submission dates)**
  - ❏ Search Engine Ranking Tool (Select One)
  - ❏ Google Search Engine Submission
  - ❏ Yahoo! Search Engine Submission
  - ❏ Bing Search Engine Submission
  - ❏ Automated XML Feed
  - ❏ Specialty Search Submission Sites
  - ❏ Other

- ❏   **STANDARD SET PRIMARY KEYWORDS/TAGS**
  - ❏ Enter at least 8
  - ❏
  - ❏
  - ❏
  - ❏
  - ❏
  - ❏
  - ❏
- ❏   **STANDARD PAGE DESCRIPTION TAG**

  Enter 150-character description, preferably including at least 4 of the keywords above

SOCIAL MEDIA SERVICES

- ❑ **Social Bookmarking Sites** (Select at least one; Enter Name, URL, Log In Info for all)
  - ❑ Delicious
  - ❑ StumbleUpon
  - ❑ Twine
  - ❑ Other
- ❑ **Social News Sites** (Select at least one; Enter Name, URL, Log In Info for all)
  - ❑ Digg
  - ❑ Reddit
  - ❑ Propeller
  - ❑ Y! Buzz
  - ❑ Other
- ❑ **Social Shopping & Specialty Bookmark Sites** (Enter Name, URL, Log In Info for all)
  - ❑ Kaboodle
  - ❑ This Next
  - ❑ StyleHive
  - ❑ Other
- ❑ **Blogging Site** (Enter Name, URL, Log In Info for all)
  - ❑ Primary blog
  - ❑ Blog directory submission site
  - ❑ Blog monitoring site
  - ❑ Blog measuring tool sites
  - ❑ Other
- ❑ **Social Networking Sites** (Select at least one; Enter Name, URL, Log In Info for all; expand rows as needed)
  - ❑ Facebook
    - ❑ Groups
    - ❑ Tools
    - ❑ Metrics
    - ❑ Follow Us On
  - ❑ Twitter
    - ❑ Groups
    - ❑ Tools
    - ❑ Metrics
    - ❑ Follow Us On
  - ❑ LinkedIn
    - ❑ Groups
    - ❑ Tools
    - ❑ Metrics
    - ❑ Follow Us On
  - ❑ MySpace
    - ❑ Groups
    - ❑ Tools
    - ❑ Metrics
    - ❑ Follow Us On
  - ❑ Google Buzz
  - ❑ Squidoo
  - ❑ Specialty Networks
  - ❑ Other Professional Networking, e.g. Plaxo
  - ❑ Other Vertical Industry Networks, e.g. DeviantArt
  - ❑ Other Demographic Networks, e.g. myYearbook
- ❑ **Social Media Sharing Sites** (Enter Name, URL, Log In Info for all)
  - ❑ YouTube
  - ❑ UStream

❏ Vimeo
❏ FlickR
❏ Picasa
❏ Podcasts
❏ Other
❏ **Social Community Sites (Enter Name, URL, Log In Info for all)**
❏ Ning
❏ Forums
❏ Message Boards
❏ Other
❏ **Other Social Media Services (Enter Name, URL, Log In Info for all)**
❏ Geolocation, e.g. Foursquare, Loopt, Gowalla
❏ Collective Shopping, e.g. Groupon
❏ Social Gaming
❏ Virtual Social
❏ Social Mobile
❏ Other

SOCIAL MEDIA METRICS
Key Performance Indicators
❏ Enter at least 8 (e.g. Traffic, CPM, CPC, Conversion Rate, ROI)
❏
❏
❏
❏
❏
❏
❏

❏ **Analytical/Statistical Tool (Select at least One: Enter Name, URL, Log In Info for all)**
❏ Google Analytics
❏ Yahoo! Analytics
❏ AWstats
❏ SociafyQ
❏ Xinu
❏ Other
❏ Advertising Metrics (Enter Name, URL, Log In Info for Each Publication)
❏ Other
❏ Other

Depending on its complexity and availability of support, think in terms of a timeline of 3 to 12 months, to allow time to complete the following steps. Estimate spending half your time in the planning phase, one-quarter in execution, and one-quarter in evaluation and modification:

1. Market research and online observation
2. Draft marketing goals, objectives, and plan

3. In-house preparation
   - Hiring, outsourcing, or selecting in-house staff
   - Training
   - Team-building
   - Writing social media policy document

4. Preparatory development tasks
   - Design
   - Content
   - Measurement plan and metric implementation
   - Social media tool selection and dashboard development
   - Set up your social media activity calendar (see Part III)
   - Programming and content modifications to existing website(s) as needed

5. Create accounts and pilot social media program

6. Evaluate pilot program, de-bug, and modify as needed

7. Launch and promote your social media campaign one service at a time

8. Measure and modify social media in a process of constant feedback and reiteration

Don't be afraid to build a pilot program — or several — into your plan to see what works.

Plan your work; work your plan.

Part III

Managing Your Cybersocial Campaign

. . . .

In This Part

▶ Scheduling social media activities

▶ Building a team

▶ Writing a social media policy

▶ Keeping it legal

▶ Protecting your brand reputation

. . . .

*A*fter you have a social media marketing plan, one
major task you face is managing the effort. If
you're the only one doing the work, the simplest —
and likely the hardest — task is making time for it.
Though social media need not carry a lot of up-front
development costs, it carries a significant cost in
labor.

In this part, we discuss how to set up a schedule to
keep your social media from draining all your available time. If you have employees, both you and your
company may benefit by delegating some of the
social media tasking to them and by supplementing
your in-house staff with limited time from outside
professionals.

For small businesses, it's always your money or your life. If you can't afford to hire help to work on social media, you carve it out of the time you've allocated to other marketing activities — unless, of course, you want to stretch your workday from 10 to 12 hours to 12 to 14 hours.

Finally, this part carries a word of precaution. Make sure that everyone posting to a social media outlet knows your policy about what is and isn't acceptable to protect the company's reputation and confidential material. As you launch your marketing boat onto the churning waters of social media, you should ensure that everyone is wearing a legal life preserver.

Managing Your Social Media Schedule

As you know from the rest of your business experience, if something isn't important enough to schedule, it never gets done. Social media, like the rest of your marketing efforts, can easily be swallowed up by day-to-day demands. You must set aside time for it and assign tasks to specific people.

Allocate a minimum of two hours per week if you're going to participate in social media, rather than set up pages and abandon them. Otherwise, you simply don't see a return from your initial investment in setup. If you don't have much time, stick with the marketing you're already doing.

Bounding the time commitment

Social media can become addictive. If you truly like what you're doing, the time problem might reverse. Rather than spend too little time, you spend too much. You might find it difficult to avoid the temptation of continually reading what others have to say about your business or spending all your time tweeting, streaming, and posting.

Just as you stick to your initial dollar budget, keep to your initial time budget, at least for the first month until you see what works. After you determine which techniques have the greatest promise, you can rearrange your own efforts, and your team's.

One way to reduce the time you spend on social media is to turn social media into part of your art, or into a product in and of itself. Of course, that strategy may not work for everyone's business.

Social media marketing is only part of your online marketing effort, and online marketing is only part of your overall marketing effort.

Selecting "activity" days

One way to control the time you spend on social media is to select specific days and times for it. Many businesspeople set aside regularly recurring blocks of time, such as on a quiet Friday afternoon, for marketing-related tasks, whether they're conducting competitor research, writing press releases or newsletters for release the following week, obtaining inbound links, or handling their social marketing tasks.

Other people prefer to allocate their time early in the morning, at lunchtime, or just before leaving work each evening. The time slot you choose usually doesn't matter, unless you're offering a time-dependent service, such as accepting to-go orders for breakfast burritos via Twitter.

> Whatever the case, use your social media activity calendar to allot time for every task; include the initials of the person responsible for executing the tasks.

Allowing for ramp-up time

Even if you're the only person involved, allow time for learning before your official social media launch date. Everyone needs time to observe, master new tools, practice posting and responding, experiment, and decide what works before rolling out a plan.

> Bring your new social media venues online one at a time. This strategy not only helps you evaluate which social media venue works but also reduces stress on you and your staff.

Developing your social date book

There are as many ways to schedule social media activities as there are companies. Whatever you decide, don't leave your schedule to chance.

Larger companies may use elaborate project management software, either proprietary solutions or open source programs such as Endeavour Software Project Management (http://endeavour-mgmt.sourceforge.net), GanttProject (www.ganttproject.biz), or OpenProj (www.serena.com/products/openproj). Alternatively, you can schedule tasks using spreadsheet software.

However, the simplest solution may be the best:
Calendaring software, much of which is free, may be
all you need. Paid options may merge schedules for
more people and allow customized report formats.
Several options are listed in Table 3-1. Look for a solution that lets you

- ✔ Choose a display by day, week, or month or
  longer.
- ✔ List events or tasks in chronological format.
- ✔ Select different timeframes easily.
- ✔ Easily schedule repeat activities without requir-
  ing duplicate data entry.

Table 3-1	Calendaring Software	
Name	**URL**	**Free or Paid**
Calendar & Time Management Software Reviews	`http://download. cnet.com/windows/ calendar-and-time- management-software`	Free, shareware, and paid
Connect Daily	`www.mhsoftware.com/ connectdaily.htm`	Paid, free trial
EventsLink Network	`www.eventslink.net`	Paid, free trial
Google Calendar	`www.google.com/ intl/en/google calendar/about.html`	Free
Mozilla Sunbird	`www.mozilla.org/ projects/calendar/ sunbird`	Free, open source

(continued)

Table 3-1 *(continued)*

Name	URL	Free or Paid
Trumba	www.trumba.com/ connect/default. aspx	Paid, free trial
Yahoo! Calendar	http://calendar. yahoo.com	Free

If several people are involved in a substantial social media effort, select calendaring software that lets you synchronize individual calendars, such as Google, Yahoo!, Mozilla Sunbird, and others. Figure 3-1 shows a sample of a simple social marketing calendar using Yahoo! The calendar shows the initials of the person responsible. Clicking an event or a task reveals item details, including the time allotted to the task, the sharing level, and whether a reminder is sent and to whom. Figure 3-2 offers an example of an event detail listing in Mozilla Sunbird.

Throughout this book, we refer to this calendar as your *Social Media Activity Calendar,* and we add frequent recommendations of tasks to include on your schedule.

Figure 3-1: Using Yahoo! Calendar, you can easily schedule your social media activities.

Set your calendar to private, but give access to everyone who needs to be aware of your social media schedule. Depending on the design of your social media program, some outside subcontractors may need access to your calendar to schedule their own production deadlines.

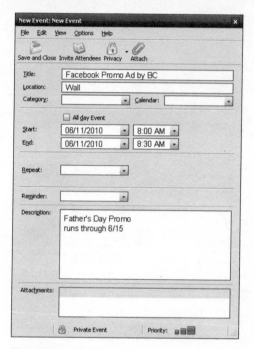

Figure 3-2: On the Sunbird event detail screen, you configure each social media task as needed.

Creating a social media dashboard

Your social media marketing efforts may ultimately involve many tasks: Post to multiple venues; use tools to distribute content to multiple locations; monitor visibility for your company on social media outlets; and measure results by using several different analytical tools. Rather than jump back and forth among all these different sources, a graphical dashboard or control panel can be a convenient timesaver.

Like the dashboard of a car, a social media dashboard puts the various required functions at your fingertips, in (you hope) an easy-to-understand and easy-to-use visual layout. When you use this approach, the customized dashboard provides easy access in one location to all your social media accounts, tools, and metrics. Figures 3-3 and 3-4 show several tabs of a customized Netvibes dashboard — one for social media postings and another for tools.

Courtesy Netvibes

Figure 3-3: This mock-up of a social media dashboard from Netvibes gathers various social media services on the first tab for a user who manages multiple accounts.

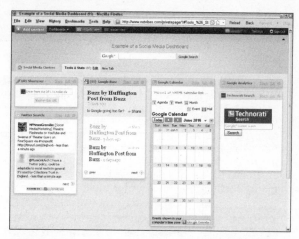

Courtesy Netvibes

Figure 3-4: The second tab of this mock-up for a Netvibes dashboard gathers tools for distributing, monitoring, searching, and analyzing.

The items on your primary dashboard may link to other, application-specific dashboards, especially for analytical tools and high-end enterprise solutions; those application dashboards are designed primarily to compare the results of multiple social media campaigns.

Table 3-2 provides a list of dashboard resources, some of which are generic (such as iGoogle and MyYahoo!) and others of which, such as Netvibes and HootSuite (see Figure 3-5), are specific to social media.

Table 3-2	**Social Media Dashboard Resources**	
Name	*URL*	*Description*
Goojet	www.goojet.com	Free mobile short-message dashboard client
HootSuite	www.hootsuite.com	Free short-message dashboard that focuses on Twitter
iGoogle	www.google.com/ig	Free, customizable Google home page
Marketing-Profs	www.marketingprofs.com/articles/2010/3454/how-to-create-your-marketing-dashboard-in-five-easy-steps	Instructions for customizing a dashboard (sign up for the free trial to view)
MyYahoo!	http://my.yahoo.com	Free, customizable Yahoo! home page
Netvibes	http://netvibes.com	Free, customizable dashboard for social media
Pageflakes	www.pageflakes.com/Default.aspx	Free, customizable dashboard

(continued)

Table 3-2 *(continued)*

Name	URL	Description
Search Engine Land	`http://search engineland.com/ b2b-social-media- dashboard-a- powerful-tool- to-uncover- key-customer- insights-17839`	Tips on how to use a social media dash- board for B2B
uberVU	`www.ubervu.com`	Paid social media dash- board client
Unilyzer	`http://unilyzer.com`	Paid social media dash- board client

Before you try to build a dashboard, list all the social media sources, services, and reports you want to dis- play, along with their associated URLs, usernames, and passwords. It will help if you indicate whether services are interconnected (for example, note if you're using a syndication service to update multiple social media at once) and how often statistical reports should be updated for each service (hourly, daily, weekly, or monthly).

The more complex the social media campaign, the more functionality the dashboard needs. For example, Natasha Wescoat's home page (`www.natasha wescoat.com`), shown in Figure 3-6, indicates that her dashboard might include controls and analytics for a Facebook fan page, her blog, and other compo- nents of the social web.

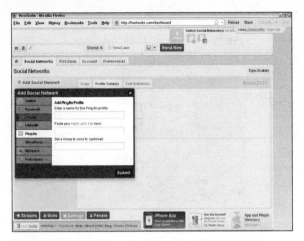

Courtesy HootSuite. The HootSuite wordmark is a trademark of HootSuite Media, Inc.
Figure 3-5: The social media dashboard from HootSuite lets you easily add social network services to your list of monitored sites.

Dashboards sound simple to use, but they can be a bit of a challenge to set up. In some cases, your programmer needs to create or customize *widgets* (mini applications). Plan to create and test several versions of the dashboard until everyone is satisfied with the results.

Consider implementing password access for approved users to various functions within the dashboard. Some users might be constrained to viewing reports whereas others might be allowed to change the dashboard configuration.

Social media

Courtesy Natasha Wescoat
Figure 3-6: The number of social media options, shown here in the lower right navigation area, affects the complexity of a dashboard.

Building Your Social Media Marketing Dream Team

Just for the moment, assume that you have employees who can — and are willing to — share the burden of social media. If you live a rich fantasy life, assume that you might even hire someone to take the lead.

In a larger company, the nexus for control of social media varies: In some cases, it's the marketing department; in others, corporate communications, public relations, sales, or customer support takes the lead.

Some companies disperse responsibilities throughout the company and have tens to dozens of people blogging and tweeting.

If your plan requires multiple employees to leverage LinkedIn profiles for B2B reasons, as well as post on multiple blogs in their individual areas of expertise and tweet current events in their departments, your need for coordination will increase.

Be cautious about asking employees to coordinate links and comments with their personal social media accounts. This task should be voluntary. Alternatively, on company time and on an account that "belongs" to your company (using a business e-mail address), ask employees to develop a hybrid personal-and-business account where their personalities can shine. Now, individual privacy and First Amendment rights are respected on their separate personal accounts, and you have no liability for the content they post there.

 No matter who does the bulk of the work — your staff members or contractors or a combination — always monitor your program randomly but regularly. In addition to getting routine reports on the results, log in to your accounts for a few minutes at various times of the day and week to see what's going on.

Seeking a skilled social director

A good social media director should have an extroverted personality. This person should truly enjoy interacting with others and take intrinsic pleasure in conversation and communication. You might want to look, based on your chosen tactics, for someone who can

- ✔ Write quickly and well, with the right tone for your market.
- ✔ Listen well, with an "ear" for your target audiences and their concerns.
- ✔ Post without using defamatory language or making libelous statements about competitors.
- ✔ Communicate knowledgeably about your company and products or services.
- ✔ Recognize opportunities and develop creative responses or campaigns.
- ✔ Work tactfully with others, alerting them when problems or complaints surface.
- ✔ Articulate the goals of social media well enough to take a leadership role in encouraging others to explore its potential.
- ✔ Analyze situations to draw conclusions from data.
- ✔ Adapt to new social media and mobile technologies as they arise.
- ✔ Learn quickly (because this field is extremely fluid).

This combination of skills, experience, and personality may be hard to find. Add to it the need to reach different submarkets for different reasons. Now you have several reasons to build a team with a leader, rather than rely on a single individual to handle all your social media needs.

You usually can't just "add" social media to someone's task list; be prepared to reassign some tasks to other people.

Depending on the size and nature of your social media effort, your dream team may also need someone with production skills for podcasting or videocasting, or at least for producing and directing the development of those components. Though this person may not need extensive graphical, photographic, presentation, or data crunching skills, having some skills in each of those areas is helpful.

Hiring twentysomethings (or younger) because they're "familiar" with social media may sound like a good idea, but people in this age group aren't as likely to be familiar with business protocol or sensitive to business relationships, as someone older and more experienced might be. You might need to allow extra time for training, review, and revision.

Looking inside

Before implementing a social media plan, speak with your employees to invite their input, assess their level of interest in this effort, evaluate existing skill sets, and ascertain social media experience. Consider all these factors before you move forward; by rearranging task assignments or priorities, you may be able to select in-house personnel to handle this new project.

 Leave time for communication, education, and training, not only at the beginning but also on an ongoing basis.

Hiring experts

Think about using professionals for the tech-heavy pieces, such as podcasts, videocasts, or design, unless you're going for the just-us-folks tone. Professionals can get you started by establishing a model for your staff to follow, or you may want to hire them for long-term tasks such as writing or editing your blogs for consistency.

Many advertising agencies, PR firms, search engine optimizers, marketing companies, and copywriters now take on social media contracts. If you've already worked with someone you like, you can start there. If not, select social media professionals the same way you would select any other professional service provider:

- ✔ Ask your local business colleagues for referrals.

- ✔ Check sources such as LinkedIn and Plaxo. If appropriate, post your search criteria on your site, blog, social media outlets, and topic-related sites.

- ✔ Request several price quotes. If your job is large enough, write and distribute a formal Request for Proposal (RFP).

- ✔ Review previous work completed by the contractors.

- ✔ Check references.

Creating a Social Media Marketing Policy

Even if you're the only person involved in social media marketing at the beginning, write up a few general guidelines for yourself that you can expand later. In Figure 3-7, the ITBusinessEdge site (www.it businessedge.com) shows a simple social media policy.

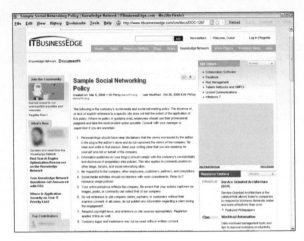

Courtesy NarrowCast Group/IT Business

Figure 3-7: A simple social media policy may be enough to get you started.

Most policies address the social media issue both in terms of what employees are allowed to do on behalf of the company and on what they aren't allowed to do. For example:

- ✔ Employees may not be allowed to use personal social accounts on company time.

- ✔ Some trained employees may be allowed to post customer support replies on behalf of the company, while others are responsible for new product information.

For additional information, see the resources listed in Table 3-3.

Table 3-3	Social Media Policy Resource Sites	
Name	**URL**	**Description**
Daniel Hoang	www.danielhoang. com/2009/02/21/ social-media- policies-and- procedures	Social media policy article
Digital Brand Expressions	www.digitalbrand expressions.com/ services/company- social-media- policy.asp	Free checklist
emTrain	www.emtrain.com/ site/page.php?p= whitepapers	Free articles and guidelines
Inc.com	www.inc.com/ articles/2010/01/ need-a-social- media-policy.html	Article titled "Do You Need a Social Media Policy?"
Mashable	http://mashable. com/2009/04/27/ social-media- policy	Article titled "Should Your Company Have a Social Media Policy?"
Mashable	http://mashable. com/2009/06/02/ social-media- policy-musts	"10 Must- Haves for Your Social Media Policy"

Name	URL	Description
Policy Tool for Social Media	`http://socialmedia.` `policytool.net`	Free social media policy generator
Social Media Govern- ance	`http://socialmedia` `governance.com/` `policies.php`	Free database of policies for review
Toolkit Café	`http://toolkitcafe.` `com/social_media_` `policies.php`	Policies toolkit ($149)

To increase compliance, keep your policy short and easy to read. Try to focus on what people *can do* rather than on what they cannot do.

A typical policy addresses risk management, intellectual property protection, individual privacy protection, and the respect of your audience, company, and fellow employees. Try to incorporate the following suggested concepts, adapted from Mashable (`http://` `mashable.com/2009/06/02/social-media-` `policy-musts`):

- ✔ Hold individuals responsible for what they write.
- ✔ Disclose who you are, including your company name and title.
- ✔ Recognize that clients, prospects, competitors, and potential future employees are part of your audience.
- ✔ Be respectful of everyone.
- ✔ Understand the tenor of each social media community and follow its precepts.

✔ Respect copyrights and trademarks.

✔ Protect your company's confidential trade secret and proprietary information in addition to client data, especially trade secret information under nondisclosure agreements.

✔ Do *not* allow personal social media activity to interfere with work.

The complexity of your social media policy depends on the extent of your social media marketing effort and the number of people and departments involved. Generally, the larger the company, the longer the policy.

Staying on the Right Side of the Law

Just about everything in social media pushes the limits of existing intellectual property law. So much information is now repeated online that ownership lines are becoming blurred, much to some people's dismay and damage.

When in doubt, don't copy. Instead, use citations, quote marks, and links to the original source. Always go back to the original to ensure that the information is accurate.

Watch blogs such as Mashable and TechCrunch for information about legal wrangling. New case law, regulations, and conflicts bubble up continually.

Obtaining permission to avoid infringement

You can't (legally) use extended content from someone else's website, blog, or social media page on your own site, even if you can save it or download it. Nope, not even if you include a credit line saying where it came from. Not even if you use only a portion of the content and link to the rest. Not text, not graphics, not compiled data, not photos. Nothing. Nada. Nil. Zilch.

Though small text extracts with attribution are permitted under fair use doctrine, the copyright concept is intended for individuals and educational institutions, not for profit-making companies. If you don't obtain permission, you and your company can be sued for copyright infringement. In the best-case scenario, you can be asked to cease and desist. In the worst case, your site can be shut down, and you might face other damages.

Be especially careful with photographs, which are usually copyrighted. Here are a few places to find free or low-cost images legally:

- ✔ Select from the wealth of material offered under a Creative Commons license (http://creativecommons.org) or copyright-free images from the federal government.

- ✔ Flickr Commons (www.flickr.com/commons) has thousands of free photographs.

- ✔ Search http://images.google.com and read the copyright information at the top of each image.

✔ Look for stock images from inexpensive sources such as iStockphoto (www.istockphoto.com), Stock Exchange (http://www.sxc.hu), or freerangestock.com.

Trademarks and logos also usually require permission to use, though the logos (icons) that social media companies provide for Share This or Follow Us On functionality are fine to use without permission. If you find an image in the Press or Media section of a company's website, you can assume that you have permission to reproduce it without further permission. Generally, a disclaimer that "all other logos and trademarks are the property of their respective owners" will suffice.

If it's illegal offline, it's illegal online.

Respecting privacy

Providing a disclaimer about keeping user information private is even more critical now that people sign up willy-nilly online. Individual privacy, already under threat, has become quite slippery with the newly released plans for making a Facebook Connect sign-in available on all sorts of third-party sites. Facebook Connect may make sign-ins simpler for a user, but it gives Facebook access to user behavior on the web while giving third parties access to users' Facebook profiles for demographic analysis.

Photographs of identifiable individuals, not taken in a public space, historically have required a waiver to use for commercial purposes. When individuals post their images on Facebook, LinkedIn, MySpace, or elsewhere, they may not intend to give permission for that image to appear elsewhere.

Respect a person's space; do not post publicly viewable images of people's faces on any of your social media pages unless you have permission. For a simple photo waiver, see www.nyip.com/ezine/techtips/model-release.html.

Revealing product endorsement relationships

Taking aim at companies that were arranging paid recommendations from bloggers (think about the deejay payola scandal of the 1950s), the Federal Trade Commission (FTC) issued new regulations in October 2009 that gave the blogosphere conniptions. The new rule requires bloggers to disclose whether they've received any type of payment or free products in exchange for a positive review.

The rule doesn't appear to apply to individuals who post a review on public review sites such as Epinions. com or TripAdvisor or Yelp, but it applies if you review other companies' products on your blog or send products to other bloggers to request a review. (In 2010, Yelp ran into other legal problems for allegedly requiring companies to buy advertising to balance the appearance of positive and negative reviews on a results page — but that's a topic for another book.)

You can find out more about this requirement from the disclosure resources listed in Table 3-4. Many bloggers, offended by the rules, have found humorous or sarcastic ways to comply; others, such as the blogger shown in Figure 3-8, are more matter-of-fact about it.

Table 3-4	Legal Resource Sites	
Name	*URL*	*Description*
American Bar Association	`www.abanet.org/ intelprop/home.html`	Intellectual property resource lists
Cases Blog	`http://casesblog. blogspot.com/2010/ 04/guidance-on- blogger-disclosure- and-ftc.html`	Blog disclosure summary
U.S. Copyright Office	`www.copyright.gov`	Copyright information and submission
Edelman Digital	`http://edelman digital.com/ 2010/03/18/sxsw- essentials- practical-guidance- on-blogger- disclosure-and- ftc-guidelines`	Blog disclosure article
Electronic Frontier Foundation	`www.eff.org`	Not-for-profit focused on free speech, privacy, and consumer rights
Federal Trade Commission	`www.ftc.gov/opa/ 2009/10/endortest. shtml`	Blog disclosure law

Name	URL	Description
FindLaw	`http://small business.findlaw. com/business- operations/small- business-internet/`	Online legal issues
International Technology Law Association	`www.itechlaw.org`	Online legal issues
Internet Legal Research Group	`www.ilrg.com`	Index of legal sites, free forms, and documents
Nolo	`http://www.nolo. com/legal- encyclopedia/ ecommerce-website- development`	Online legal issues
United States Patent and Trademark Office	`www.uspto.gov`	Patent and trademark information, databases, and submission
Word of Mouth Marketing Association	`http://womma.org/ ethics/disclosure`	Blog disclosure article

Courtesy 15 Minute Beauty Fanatic

Figure 3-8: The blogger sets out a clear acknowledgment policy on product endorsement.

> Regardless of what you think of the policy, reveal any payments or free promotional products you've received. You can, of course, be as clever, funny, cynical, or straightforward as you want.

Protecting Your Brand

The three important aspects to protecting your brand online are copyright protection, trademark protection, and brand reputation.

Copyrighting your material

Copyright protects creative work in any medium — text, photos, graphics, audio, video, multimedia, software — from being used by others without permission or payment. Your work becomes your intellectual property as soon as you've created it in a fixed form. The rules for copyright are simple: Protect your own work and don't use other people's work without permission.

Whenever you sign an agreement with a subcontractor, especially a photographer, to create original work for your website, social media pages, or other advertising venue, read the contract to determine who will own the copyright on the work they create. In most cases, you can stipulate that their efforts constitute a work-for-hire arrangement, so the copyright belongs to you. (Photographers may give you only a limited license to use their creative work in one application.)

Your employee agreement should clearly state that your company retains ownership of any intellectual property that employees create for you. This area gets interesting if employees post things about your company on their personal social media accounts. It's another reason, if you needed one, for creating a hybrid personal/business account.

Put a copyright notice on your website. The standard format includes the word *copyright* or *copr* or the symbol © followed by the year, name of copyright holder, and, usually, the term *All Rights Reserved.* The easiest way to do this is in the footer so that it appears on every page. Here's an example you can incorporate into your website, blog, or other uniquely created material:

```
© 2010 Watermelon Mountain Web Marketing
All rights reserved.
```

This common law copyright notice informs other people that the material is copyrighted and gives you basic protections. For more protection, file officially at www.copyright.gov. Basic online submissions start at only $35. Copyright is usually easy enough to file yourself, but call the copyright office or your attorney if you have questions.

You cannot copyright ideas or titles.

Trademarking your brand names

Trademarks (for goods) or *service marks* (for services) give you the exclusive right to use a particular name or logotype within specific commercial categories. You can trademark your own name, if you want, and you must acknowledge the trademarks and service marks of others. The first time you use a trademarked name (including your own) in text on your site, follow it with the superscript ® for a registered mark or ™ for a pending mark that hasn't yet been issued. Provide a notice of trademark ownership somewhere on your site.

Trademark rights apply online. For instance, only the trademark owner has the legal right to register a domain name with that trademark. The same constraint applies to celebrity names. If you think a competitor is infringing one of your trademarks, see your intellectual property (IP) or business attorney.

Fees for online filing start at $275 but depend on which form you must file. Filing a trademark is a bit more complicated than filing a copyright application. For directions, see the trademark section of the United States Patent and Trademark Office site (www.uspto.gov/trademarks/index.jsp). Check the trademark database (http://tess2.uspto.gov) for availability of the trademark within your class of goods or services, and then follow the prompts. Though you can legally submit a trademark application yourself, you might want to call an IP attorney for help.

 Filing a patent is much more difficult, and much more expensive, than filing a trademark. Be sure to consult an IP attorney for patent filings.

Protecting your brand reputation

Start protecting your brand now by registering your name for social media accounts. To avoid "brandjacking," try to choose the most popular, available "handle" that will work across multiple sites. Use your company or product name and keep it short.

 Even if you don't plan to do anything else in social media for a year or more, register your name now on Facebook, Twitter, LinkedIn, and on any other sites you might want in the future, such as Flickr, MySpace, or YouTube. You can do this on every site as you read this book or reserve them all now.

A number of companies now offer tools that claim to assess the "quality" of what people are saying about your company, products, or staff. In addition to counting how many times your name appears, they try to assess the "sentiment" of postings — whether statements are negative or positive. Some also offer an assessment of the degree of engagement — how enthusiastic or hostile a statement might be.

Some people then take this information, along with frequency of posting, and use their own, proprietary formulas to assign a quantitative value to your online reputation, as shown in the example in Figure 3-9.

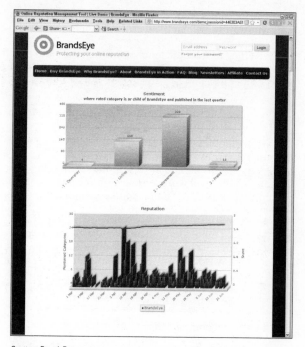

Courtesy BrandsEye

Figure 3-9: BrandsEye offers an inexpensive "reputation" management tool that scales up for larger users.

Be cautious about assigning too much weight to these brand reputation tools. They may produce widely varying results, and most rely on software that cannot understand complex sentences or shortened phrases with words omitted. If you think your dense sibling doesn't understand irony, don't try sarcasm with a computer!

Part IV

Joining the Conversation

- -

In This Part

▶ Lurking and listening

▶ Minding your online manners

▶ Keeping your audience engaged

- -

1 t takes some practice to discern relevant information when you first skim the flow of a stream of
comments on Facebook or Twitter. Even when you
join a threaded discussion in a group or reply to a
blog, you're stepping into an already running river
of information and relationships.

It seems obvious that the first step is to "get your
bearings," just as you would at a conference or party.
You can, almost intuitively, assess how many people
are present, who they are, how they behave, the
emotional tone of the event, and who or what is
the center of attention.

Yet many people start gabbing online before they truly
grasp what's going on in that particular little corner
of cyberspace. Whichever social networking methods
you've chosen, start by watching and learning for at
least a few days before you contribute. Unless you
have unlimited time, select only a few groups, people,
or companies to observe in each venue.

Each form of social media has its own search tools. Search for competitors, keywords, topics, and groups that are relevant to your business. Google Search now also incorporates social media. To sort for those results, click Show Options in the upper-left corner of any search results page; then select Updates in the left navigation area. Results from recent posts on social media feeds are displayed.

After you decide whom to follow or which groups to join, you can incorporate the principles in this part to gain invaluable market intelligence and become a valued participant in an ongoing conversation.

Lurking and Listening

You don't have to make detailed charts, but you should pay attention to several factors as you decide whether a specific account is worth following or whether a particular group is worth your time:

- ✔ The frequency and quantity of comments on a particular topic

- ✔ The length of a typical post

- ✔ Who posts and who receives the most responses

- ✔ The content of the posts and their relevance to your needs

- ✔ The quality of the posts and the value of the information they provide

- ✔ The tone of the communication

- ✔ The ratio of wheat (relevant to you) to chaff (nonrelevant to you)

Recognize that your goal isn't to become the center of attention, but rather to understand the concerns and interests of your target market, to build relationships, and to establish a reputation for your business. Social media conversations are much more about marketing than about sales.

Recall the old aphorism "You have two ears and one mouth because you should listen twice as much as you talk." That's a good rule to follow for your participation on social media. If in doubt, listen more.

Listening actively

The most important part of any offline conversation isn't the talking; it's the listening. The same concept is true online. You can easily apply active listening techniques to social media. If you're good at sales, you may already use this approach intuitively to understand the underlying problem that a prospective customer is trying to solve.

When you're online, you don't have the luxury of non-verbal cues, such as tone of voice and body language, but you can still pay careful attention to the words on the page and any unstated concerns that may underlie them. The steps for your reply are simple:

1. Thank people for their interest or for bringing up their concern.

2. Repeat the key element of their post in their own words.

3. Ask nonjudgmental questions for clarification, paraphrasing their point or concern. Try to detect an underlying emotional quality to which you can relate or respond.

4. When you're ready to answer with your own point of view, give an example or tell a story. Try to incorporate their point, restated in your own words.

5. Invite further response.

In some cases, you're better off extending a conversation with multiple back-and-forth posts than trying to accomplish all these goals in one message.

Active listening works best when you're sincerely interested in what someone else has to say.

Hearing an opportunity and taking it

The social media world is replete with examples of someone who was truly listening and took an action that made a difference. In many cases, that action resulted in invaluable word-of-mouth recommendations and, in some cases, publicity worth more than any paid advertising.

For instance, FreshBooks, a Canadian-based online billing and bookkeeping service (www.freshbooks.com) with more than a million clients, is a committed user of Twitter (http://twitter.com/freshbooks). One evening in May 2008, an alert employee noticed a stream of tweets from a FreshBooks customer describing how she had been stood up for a date. FreshBooks not only tweeted a message, shown at the top of Figure 4-1, but also sent the client a bouquet of flowers.

The surprised client blogged and tweeted her delight, resulting in hundreds of devoted followers for FreshBooks. The company now gathers from its Twitter feed remarkable insight into problems and requested product features. The gesture by FreshBooks earned it the loyalty of hundreds of volunteer product evangelists who now help with online tech support, reducing the cost of calls to the FreshBooks customer support center. All this was a result of empathizing with a customer's feelings.

Others have followed in the footsteps of FreshBooks. Targus, Inc., an international manufacturer of computer cases and accessories, uses its Twitter account (http://twitter.com/targus_inc) as an inexpensive way to build brand loyalty and increase its number of fans. It frequently offers special giveaways and promotions to its Twitter followers and monitors conversations to discover prospects who are close to a purchase.

Careful attention to the Twitter stream identified a conversation involving someone who had purchased a bag from a competitor and wasn't happy with it. Targus sent him a coupon code for 25 percent off, as shown at the bottom of Figure 4-1. Again, the happy customer wrote others about his experience, became a long-term loyal client, and yielded valuable word-of-mouth recommendations.

(Top) Courtesy FreshBooks; (Bottom) Courtesy Targus Inc.
Figure 4-1: FreshBooks followed up this famous tweet to a client with a bouquet of flowers (top). Targus tweeted an online promo code to a prospective customer (bottom).

The secret to success in each case is being alert, attentive, and responsive.

A curious and media-savvy operations manager was already using Twitter in October 2008 to build up the clientele for the Houston coffee shop The Coffee Groundz (http://coffeegroundz.net). When he received what is now recognized as the first "to-go" order on Twitter, he responded as though it were the most natural thing in the world (see Figure 4-2). Now that the Library of Congress is archiving the entire repertoire of Twitter messages, these two will probably end up on display!

Soon, The Coffee Groundz was accepting Twitter pre-orders from all its clientele, which has since doubled from all the attention. Continuing its love affair with social media, the business hosts numerous Houston tweet-ups and foursquare events — proof, perhaps, that good things come to those who listen.

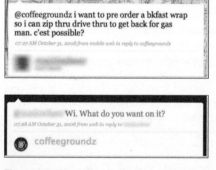

Figure 4-2: When The Coffee Groundz in Houston received the world's first tweeted to-go order, on the top, it responded immediately, as shown on the bottom.

Minding Your Social Media P's & Q's

The more the technology changes, the more technology stays the same. Common courtesy and common sense will get you far. The old rules of netiquette apply to social media, whether you're blogging, tweeting, commenting in a LinkedIn group, or posting to your Facebook stream.

Keeping these points in mind keeps your social capital high:

- ✔ **Be subtle, not self-promotional in your posts.** Avoid blatant advertising.

- ✔ **Content is king.** Whatever the venue, freely contribute real information. Share resources, connections, and links with other members of the community.

- ✔ **Avoid using ALL CAPITAL letters in any post.** It's considered "shouting."

- ✔ **Avoid e-mailing individuals directly.** This advice applies unless they have requested a personal response.

- ✔ **Respect your audience.** Avoid negative comments, name-calling, and expletives. "If you can't say something nice, don't say anything at all."

If your powers of observation aren't enough to detect the unwritten rules or customs for each of the various networking options, the social media etiquette resources listed in Table 4-1 can help.

Table 4-1	Some Social Media Etiquette Resources	
Name	*URL*	*Article Title*
Forbes magazine	www.forbes.com/2009/10/09/social-networking-etiquette-entrepreneurs-management-wharton.html	Are You Practicing Proper Social Networking Etiquette?
DaniWeb.com	www.daniweb.com/news/story220189.html#	@Miss Manners — Social Media Etiquette
Community Organizer 2.0	www.communityorganizer20.com/2009/01/12/social-media-etiquette-roundup-understanding-cultural-norms	Social Media Etiquette Roundup: Understanding Cultural Norms
Techipedia	www.techipedia.com/2008/social-media-etiquette-handbook	The Ultimate Social Media Etiquette Handbook

Sticking to business

Though some social media-istas encourage writing from a personal framework, that strategy may get you into trouble. The line between being personable and being personal is so faint that it's often hard to follow. You can generally talk safely about your personal evaluation of a product or event or share work-related information about business contacts you met at a trade show, but keep intimate information about your personal friends and children on your personal, friends-only blog.

It's fine to include a brief notice that no one will be tweeting for a week. But don't post that picture of you sipping a drink with a little paper umbrella or riding a surfboard on your social media pages (unless, of course, you're in the business of drinks with paper umbrellas, or surfboards, or travel).

When you become too chatty, you may inadvertently disclose private information about someone else or information that truly is company-confidential. If you feel you must disclose this type of information to a particular prospect, for goodness' sake, use a direct e-mail or, better, the phone. Request a signed nondisclosure agreement before discussing any proprietary or trade secret information!

 Do not disclose confidential, proprietary, personnel, or trade secret information. Duh! If you aren't certain what to disclose, just review or revise your company policy.

Selling them softly with your song

Some businesses experiment with hard-core sales promotions, making their feeds nothing more than a continuous stream of ads. Though this strategy might make sense for a coupon distribution site such as http://twitter.com/mommysavers, it doesn't make sense for most B2B businesses or service companies.

There are many ways to reduce the promotional density with other content, especially on Facebook and Twitter:

✔ Include industry news in your feeds.

✔ Increase the frequency of your responses to posts from followers.

✔ Include news and teasers about new products and about appearances at trade shows or craft fairs, or describe how you find new lines to carry or manufacture.

✔ Cultivate a circle of friends in related businesses whose news you can retweet; celebrate achievements, share business suggestions; and encourage each other, as Rotem Gear does with its Twitter feed at `http://twitter.com/jrotem`, shown in Figure 4-3.

Courtesy R. Jean Roth / Rotem Design Studio

Figure 4-3: Rotem Gear balances a tweet about its own product line with messages to business colleagues.

✔ If your company donates to a nonprofit organization, talk about the cause that you believe in and fundraisers related to the organization, whether it's animal welfare, breast cancer, hunger, planned parenthood, or saving the rain forest.

Engaging Your Audience

Whether you're blogging or tweeting or posting on Facebook, grabbing — and holding — readers' attention is extremely difficult. The competition is fierce. Nothing succeeds like originality, humor, and meaningful content. Of course, it's an extremely difficult order to fulfill.

Look at the "most popular" writers and posts on different social media. Try to discern the factor that's attracting readers. Use the internal search function for each social media to find people who post in a topic area; focus on those with high numbers of readers or fans.

Keeping it short and sweet

Except for followers of news and educational sites, most readers are looking for short, quick snippets of information. The snippets don't have to be as short as a tweet, but try to avoid long posts, even on your blog. Instead, use multiple short posts on multiple days and link to your hub website for more information.

For instance, break the content of a white paper into multiple blog posts of no more than several screens (about 500 words maximum). After each one, provide a link to obtain your complete white paper, for which you can request registration.

Keeping your posts short and sweet is likely to improve your search engine ranking as well as traffic.

Finding your voice

When you read something by Hemingway or Austen, you know immediately who wrote it. (If only we all had that gift.) Writers may spend years searching for their unique "voices." Every once in a while, you run across someone with a truly creative and original voice — and you know it when you see it.

Heather Gorringe, the founder and creative force behind Wiggly Wigglers (www.wigglywigglers.co.uk), has just that kind of voice. Take a look at her blog at www.wigglywigglers.blogspot.com, shown in Figure 4-4, or listen to the podcasts on her website at www.wigglywigglers.co.uk/podcasts/index.html.

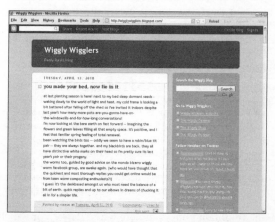

Courtesy Heather Gorringe, Wiggly Wigglers

Figure 4-4: The founder of Wiggly Wigglers has an earthy, humorous, accessible, and appealing "voice" on her blog.

Staying Engaged

Sometimes the trick to keeping customers engaged is simply to luck into (or plan for) a topic on which people have plenty of opinions. Then let 'er rip. Sometimes you don't have to comment often; just watch and observe.

You're engaged in social media conversations for the long haul. Try not to drop a thread that has had lots of comments.

For example, people debated for more than a year on the blog My Starbucks Idea (http://mystarbucks idea.force.com) about the benefits and downsides of Starbucks' use of compact fluorescent lights. A franchise operator, not Starbucks, initiated the topic, but it caught on. The posting public maintained the thread with little input from Starbucks for about 17 months.

If you're interested in the complete transcript, see http://mystarbucksidea.force.com/ ideaView?id=087500000004CnkAAE.

This list describes what Starbucks did so well. Try to emulate its work in your social media channels:

✔ **Praise commenters.** In the entry on August 12, 2009 (which concludes the chain), Sue from the Starbucks Global Responsibility department explains which actions the company has decided to take on store lighting and credits blog commenters by saying "with an update to this great idea." She adds other phrases that reflect to readers both the advantages and disadvantages they raised in their postings.

✔ **Show commenters that they're important to you.** In one entry, Jim Hanna, the head of environmental affairs, introduces himself. Having a department head respond gives greater credibility to the answer and implies, "This comment is important enough that someone with authority is responding." He is answering for the company, not in his personal role.

✔ **Give follow-up explanations with no defensiveness or derision.** Hanna thanks everyone for their posts and the good points they made, validating their input. He simply ignores the crankier posts. Carefully responding to each issue in turn, Hanna explains how Starbucks is addressing it. He makes every point positively, but not defensively. When providing explanatory material, Hanna avoids a patronizing tone. He concludes by describing the Starbucks decision-making process, leaving the floor open to additional comments.

You might want to set up your blog to review all posts before publishing so that you can remove any highly objectionable material. However, don't set the filter so high that you remove any negative or critical comments, which would quickly shut off the conversation.

Asking questions . . .

If you don't happen to have readers who are as engaged as the ones at Starbucks (see the preceding section), you can easily encourage responses. At the end of each primary post, ask readers for their opinions by posing open-ended questions. Avoid questions that prompt a simple yes-or-no answer. Here are some examples of helpful ways to ask these questions:

- ✔ What do you think about this topic, or how do you feel about this topic?
- ✔ How would you handle a certain situation?
- ✔ What's your opinion about this topic?
- ✔ What's your experience with this widget? or How would you rate this widget? Why?
- ✔ Will you share your story about a certain topic?
- ✔ What are you doing or working on now in this area?
- ✔ How would you improve it?
- ✔ What ideas do you have to solve this problem?

. . . *and answering questions*

Some topics truly lend themselves to a question-and-answer format. You can repurpose questions submitted by readers and customers, and present them in your blog, Twitter, and Facebook entries. For example, the blog for K9 Cuisine, an online retailer of dog food, has a panel of experts handle the enormous range of questions that bedevil dog owners at http://blog.k9cuisine.com, shown in Figure 4-5. It's a helpful way to distribute content from multiple points of view while sharing the workload involved in maintaining a blog.

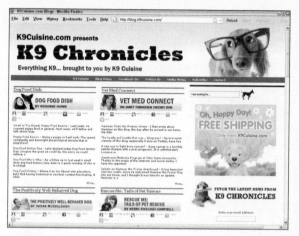

Courtesy K9Cuisine.com

Figure 4-5: K9Cuisine.com has eight different contributors on its blog, which is set up as a topic index.

Being helpful

Sometimes the simplest posts are best. Readers may often need only straightforward information. The best thing to do is supply it, as Milwaukee Electric Tool does on its Facebook page (www.facebook. com/MilwaukeeElectricTool), shown in Figure 4-6.

Courtesy Milwaukee Electric Tool

Figure 4-6: Milwaukee Electric Tool responds to customer inquiries that simply require information.

Finding content

Every once in a while, the creative well simply runs dry. Try as you might, you can't figure out what in the world to write about. Try some of the sources listed in Table 4-2 for ideas. If you're truly stuck, look around for a guest contributor to take over for a couple weeks until your juices start flowing again. Or, consider hiring a professional copywriter to help you, perhaps on a long-term basis.

Table 4-2	Blog Writing Resources	
Name	*URL*	*What You Can Find*
BLOGBloke	www.blog bloke.com/ blogging-by-osmosis	Blog-writing resources and tips
Copyblogger	www.copy blogger.com	Copywriting tips for online marketing success
ProBlogger	www.pro blogger.net	Blogging tips for bloggers
Direct Creative Blog	www.direct creative.com/ blog/writing-resources	Quick online writing resources
Smashing magazine	www.smashing magazine.com/ 2009/06/ 28/50-free-resources-that-will-improve-your-writing-skills	Free online writing resources
Vivid Image	www.vimm.com/ wp-content/ uploads/2009/ 07/50-Sources-of-Inspiration-for-Blog-Content.pdf	Fifty sources of inspiration for blog content
Writers Write	www.writers write.com/ blogging	Blogging news, resources, tools, and articles

If you decide to use contributors or contractors to write your blog, monitor their postings randomly for accuracy and tone.

Goofing with grace

Stay positive, even when you make a mistake. Graciously thanking a follower for correcting your error and moving on is more gracious than getting involved in defense of your position. If a reader's facts are incorrect, of course, gently call attention to the discrepancy, perhaps with a link to a third-party source.

 Some mistakes are minor enough that you should simply ignore them. You don't want your readers to feel that they will be criticized or corrected for every post they make. That's a total turnoff!

Handling critics

One of the trickiest problems for any writer is handling conflicts and critics. For an example, see the e-mail exchange at www.huffingtonpost.com/2010/03/08/personal-responsibilty-v_n_489822.html between Arthur Delaney, a blogger for The Huffington Post, and a reader who took issue with an article about foreclosures, evictions, and bailouts, topics sure to stir emotional embers. The exchange, which took multiple responses to reach a conclusion, took place as a series of direct, private e-mails. This discussion illustrates several good points about how to handle criticism:

✔ Try not to be defensive, and acknowledge the value of another party's point of view.

✔ If the criticism is correct, thank the writer for their input and make the correction public.

✔ If you need clarification, ask the critic to explain himself or herself further.

✔ Use facts, not emotions in your response.

✔ Persist until a point of clarity is reached, even if it's nothing more than agreeing to disagree.

✔ Sometimes it's better to resolve an issue via e-mail, which remains between two parties, instead of conducting a public disagreement. Use your judgment and discretion.

Part V

Discovering Helpful Tech Tools

· ·

In This Part

▶ Learning more about social media

▶ Distributing content efficiently

▶ Keeping search engines in the loop

▶ Giving long URLs a haircut

▶ Selecting shopping tools that work with social media

· ·

*T*he key to social media success is planning. As you select tools and schedule tasks, enter your choices on your Social Media Marketing Plan and Social Media Activity Calendar.

Try to select one or more tools from each of these categories:

✔ Resource, news, and blog sites that cover online marketing and social media

✔ Content distribution tools

✔ Tools for notifying search engines and directories of updates

✔ URL clipping tools

✔ Shopping widgets for social media

✔ Buzz-tracking tools to monitor mentions of your business

Fortunately, all these tools are online, so you don't have to lug them around!

You can always jump right into the social media scene and figure out these things later, but your efforts will be more productive if you build the right framework first.

Keeping Track of the Social Media Scene

Unless you take advantage of online resources, you'll never be able to stay current with the changes in social media. Within the space of several weeks in early 2010, for instance, Google deployed its new social networking site, Google Buzz (www.google.com/buzz), companies acquired each other, and NBC, together with Stamen Design, launched the NBC Olympics Twitter Tracker (http://bits.blogs.nytimes.com/2010/02/19/a-visual-tool-to-track-olympic-tweets/?scp=2&sq=Twitter%20Tracker&st=cse), a visual representation of the popularity of events based on the overall number of tweets submitted by individual users, shown in Figure 5-1. You can view the video at www.youtube.com/watch?v=1Rl92Q1IJ0w&feature=player_embedded.

You might want to subscribe to feeds about social marketing from one or more social marketing blogs or news services or make a habit of checking at least one of them weekly. You might also want to review traffic trends on various social media services weekly; they're amazingly volatile.

Courtesy NBC Universal

Figure 5-1: The NBC Olympics Twitter Tracker ran in real time, with video images updated continually as the frequency of tweets varied on different tags.

Include the names of resource sites on your Social Media Marketing Plan and schedule weekly research as a task on your Social Media Activity Calendar.

Saving Time with Content Distribution Tools

Social media marketing obviously can quickly consume all your waking hours and then some. Just the thought of needing to post information quickly to

Facebook, Twitter, LinkedIn, social bookmarks, blogs, Flickr, or social news services might make any social marketer cringe.

Fortunately, some tools enable you to post your content to all these places at once. You can choose from many good applications for a distribution tool:

- ✔ **Routine maintenance:** Use a content distribution tool whenever you make updates according to your Social Media Activity Calendar. What a timesaver!

- ✔ **Quick event postings:** If you want to share information from a conference, trade show, meeting, or training session, you can use most of these distribution tools from your phone to send short text updates to Twitter and LinkedIn. Or, take a picture with your cellphone and send it to Flickr and Facebook. If you want to send something longer, simply use a distribution tool to e-mail your post to your blog and Facebook.

- ✔ **Daily updates:** Group all social media services that you might want to update with rapidly changing information, such as a daily sale or the location of your traveling cupcake cart by the hour.

In addition to Ping.fm, OnlyWire, and other tools described in the next few sections, you can use Real Simple Syndication (RSS) to feed content to users and to your various social media profiles.

If you have more than three social media outlets or frequently update your content, choosing at least one distribution tool is a "must-have" way to save time.

Reconfigure your settings on Ping.fm or other content distribution tools whenever you decide to add or drop a social media service, or create a new, special purpose group for marketing purposes.

Ping.fm by Seesmic

Ping.fm, shown in Figure 5-2, lets you update some or all your social media sites at one time, for free, and without needing technical help. What's more, you don't have to be at your office computer to do it. You can send text and images from various devices, including your cellphone, e-mail program, instant messaging program, or Skype.

Courtesy Ping.fm by Seesmic
Figure 5-2: The Dashboard page for Ping.fm distributes a posting of a particular type to your selected social media services.

Ping.fm posts your updates to whichever social media services you have preselected. You can specify which types of messages go to which services (for example, photos to Flickr and short messages to Twitter).

In the Ping.fm Dashboard (http://ping.fm/dashboard), you select the destination services you want. If you don't want everything to go

everywhere, you simply create groups to determine
who gets what. Other tools operate in a similar manner.

Ping.fm posts to many social media services,
but it may not include some of your desired
specialty destinations. Try selecting Custom
URL from the Ping.fm network page. If this URL
points to a script that can accept Ping.fm messages, you're all set. Otherwise, you might need
a secondary service or RSS feed to accommo-
date everything on your list.

Although you can see a history of your postings,
Ping.fm doesn't let you track results on these services.
For that task, you can use the monitoring tools
described later in this part.

Alternative content distribution services

You have other choices for content distribution to
social media services. They all work roughly the same
as Ping.fm, but each has its own peculiarities. Choose
the one that's the best fit for you.

HelloTxt

According to the HelloTxt dashboard (`http://hello
txt.com/dashboard`), HelloTxt updates 50 services
but doesn't allow you to create groups for different
types of content. However, you can add hash tags
(# tag) to help your postings end up in the right
categories on the destination services. As with
Ping.fm, you can update by instant message, e-mail,
and text message.

HootSuite

Self-described as "the professional Twitter client,"
HootSuite (`http://hootsuite.com`) functions
primarily as a way to manage your entire Twitter

experience — from scheduling to stats — from one location. However, it now integrates Twitter, Facebook, LinkedIn, and Ping.fm accounts for multiservice postings with one submission.

OnlyWire

OnlyWire (http://onlywire.com) updates as many as 33 services simultaneously, and it's the only tool listed in this section that passes updates to your own website or blog via a content management system. You'll need to implement the OnlyWire API (Application Programming Interface) or ask your programmer to do it for you.

OnlyWire also offers two handy bookmarklets:

- ✔ A toolbar add-in to submit to OnlyWire with one click from your own browser.

- ✔ A customizable Bookmark & Share button that lets users share your site with all their own accounts at one time. OnlyWire offers the choice of an ad-supported free version or a paid service for $3 per month or $25 per year.

Posterous

Posterous (http://posterous.com) has a unique approach: You e-mail your text, photo, video, or audio files to Post@Posterous.com and it automatically creates a blog page or appends your material. Then it autoposts your content to as many as 26 social media and video services. You can specify posting to only a subset by e-mailing to a different address (http://posterous.com/manage/#autopost) or specify an e-mail address for a service that it doesn't ordinarily support. Posterous also handles RSS subscriptions and integrates with Google Analytics for statistical tracking.

TweetDeck

If you love Twitter, this content distribution tool might be the one for you. TweetDeck allows you to control much of your social media campaign through Twitter. Among its many capabilities, TweetDeck lets you update Facebook, MySpace, LinkedIn, Google Buzz, foursquare, and other social networks directly from Twitter (www.tweetdeck.com/features/update-in-a-click/index.htmltweetdeck.com). You can update your status, post comments, upload photos or videos, and follow friends' activities on these other sites from the TweetDeck control panel.

Putting Real Simple Syndication (RSS) to work

It almost sounds quaint, but RSS technology, which has been around for a decade, is still a viable way to distribute (syndicate) information for publication in multiple locations. The familiar orange-and-white icon shown in Figure 5-3 gained prominence about five years ago as a way to notify others automatically about often-updated content such as headlines, blogs, news, or music. The RSS icon indicates that a site offers a Real Simple Syndication feed.

Figure 5-3: The RSS icon.

The published content, or *feed*, is provided for free in a standardized format that can be viewed in many different programs. RSS feeds are read on the receiving end in an RSS reader, a feed reader, or an aggregator. Readers come in three species: standalone, like FeedDemon; add-ons that are compatible with specific applications; or web-based, like Mozilla Firefox's Live Bookmarks, which adds RSS feeds to a user's Favorites folder.

Feeds may be delivered to an individual subscriber's desktop, e-mail program, or browser favorites folder, or they can be reproduced on another website, blog page, or social media page.

You can offer an RSS feed from your site, blog, or social media pages (or display your own or others' RSS feeds on your pages). This feature requires some technical skills; if you're not technically inclined, ask your programmer to handle the implementation.

Subscribing is easy: Users simply click the RSS icon and follow directions. After that, the RSS reader regularly checks the list of subscribed feeds and downloads any updates. Users can receive automatic alerts or view their updates on demand. The provided material is usually a linkable abstract or headline, along with the publisher's name and date of publication. The link opens the full article or media clip.

Subscribers not only receive timely updates from their favorite sites but also can use RSS to collect feeds from many sites in one convenient place. Rather than check multiple websites every day, for instance, political junkies can have RSS feeds about Congress delivered automatically from *The Huffington Post, The Nation, The Washington Post,* and *The New York Times.*

Unless you're targeting a market that's highly proficient technically, be cautious about using RSS as your only option for sharing content. Recent studies have found that more than 12 times the number of people will subscribe to an e-mail newsletter than to an RSS feed, except in technology fields. The general public sees RSS as too technical or complicated.

 Be sure to enter your choices for content distribution on your Social Media Marketing Plan, and create a schedule for distributing updates (daily? weekly? monthly?) on your Social Media Activity Calendar.

RSS offers a distinct advantage for sharing site content with readers: one-time-and-forget-about-it installation. After RSS is installed on your site or blog, you don't have to do anything except update your master site. You don't even have to type an entry as you do with the other content distribution tools. Everyone who subscribes gets your feed automatically; you know that they're prequalified prospects because they've opted in.

From a user's point of view, RSS means that after requesting a feed, the user doesn't have to go anywhere or do anything to receive updates — updates arrive at their fingertips.

 Unfortunately, RSS coordinates with social media distribution services only if you (or your programmer) enable your other social media pages to accept and display your RSS feed. Alternatively, that person might be able to use a tool such as the OnlyWire API to program your RSS feed to accept updates for distribution to social media.

Notifying Search Engines about Updates

Some people think that search engines, especially Google, know everything about everybody's websites all the time. Not so. Even the Google grandmaster needs a tip now and again. Though all search engines routinely crawl or spider (visit and scan) websites to keep their own results current and relevant, your cycle for updates won't necessarily match their cycles for crawling.

Keeping search engines updated is valuable: Your site is not only more likely to appear in relevant search results but its ranking will also improve from frequent updates.

The solution, *pinging,* is a simple way to get the attention of search engines and directories whenever you update your blog or website. Pinging has several other uses online: to confirm that a site or server is operating; as a diagnostic tool for connectivity problems; or to confirm that a particular IP address exists.

Don't confuse the type of pinging that notifies search engines of changes to your site or blog with Ping.fm, the tool for distributing content to multiple social media services.

Pinging can be done on demand with a third-party service, or you can configure your blog, Squidoo lens, RSS feed, and some other sites to do it automatically. Generally, you simply enter the name of your blog or post your URL, select your destination(s), and click the Submit button, as shown in Figure 5-4. The service then broadcasts a message that your site contains a new post or other content.

Courtesy Rentex™

Figure 5-4: FeedPing offers pinging services for blogs and RSS feeds with an easy user interface.

Select only one service. Search engines don't take kindly to "double pinging."

WordPress, TypePad, Blogger, and most other blog services offer built-in, automatic pinging every time you post. On some smaller blog hosts, you may have to set up pinging (or submit to search engines) in a control panel.

Be sure to enter your choices for a pinging service on your Social Media Marketing Plan. If pinging isn't automatic, enter a task item for pinging below each update on your Social Media Activity Calendar.

Snipping Ugly URLs

The last thing you need when microblogging on sites such as Twitter is a URL that takes up half your

140-character limit! Long, descriptive URLs that are useful for search engines are also messy in e-mail, text messages, text versions of e-newsletters, and blogs, not to mention making it difficult to re-tweet within the limit. The solution is to snip, clip, nip, trim, shave, or otherwise shorten ungainly URLs with a URL truncating service. Take your choice of those in Table 5-1 or search for others.

Table 5-1	URL Snipping Services	
Service Name	*URL*	*Notes*
10 Short URL Services Face Off	`http://www.makeuseof.com/tag/short-url-truncators`	Comparison review article
bit.ly	`http://bit.ly/pages/about`	Popular for Twitter, free and paid versions with history, stats, and preferences
is.gd	`www.is.gd`	Users can find out where a short URL points
Ow.ly	`http://ow.ly/url/shorten-url`	HootSuite's URL shortener
Snipurl	`http://snipurl.com`	Stores, manages, and tracks traffic on short URLs
TinyURL	`http://tinyurl.com`	One of the oldest and best-known truncators

The downside is that the true owner of shortened URLs may be a mystery, so it doesn't do much for your branding. Figure 5-5 shows a typical URL truncating service and the result.

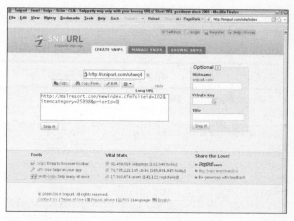

Courtesy SnipURL and Mountain Springs Lake Resort (MSLresort.com)

Figure 5-5: Enter a long URL at SnipURL and receive a short URL in exchange.

As always, enter the name of your URL snipping service on your Social Media Marketing Plan. To make it easier to track URLs and their snipped versions, select just one service.

Using E-Commerce Tools for Social Sites

If money makes the world go round, e-commerce takes the cybersocial world for a dizzying spin. You have many different options for promoting or linking to your online store from blogs and social networks, but in most cases you can't sell directly. Either the platforms don't support transactions or selling would violate the terms of service.

 Always check the terms of service on social media sites to be sure you aren't violating their rules.

Instead, most e-commerce tools display items on your blog or social profile and then link to a third-party application or an existing Webstore to complete the transaction.

Indeed, the easiest way to sell from social networks and blogs is simply to post a banner or text link to your own website or to other sites that sell your products. Composer and intuitive counselor Max Highstein does this successfully on the Meditations tab of his Facebook site (www.facebook.com/pages/The-Healing-Waterfall/111483778861659), shown in Figure 5-6. Each meditation links to the primary website store (www.guidedimagerydownloads.com) for down-loads and payment. Omelle does something similar in Figure 5-7, using shortened links in its Twitter stream to take visitors directly to its on-site store.

E-commerce widgets are mini-displays of products in your store; these changeable badges link to a real cyberstore. If you already have an online store, check your own shopping cart or check-stand provider to see if it offers a widget for social media, too.

 Many vendors offer customers the equivalent widget functionality for use on some compatible social media services. For instance, Zazzle.com offers a Merch Store application for Facebook and Merchbook widget for MySpace; PayPal offers one for TypePad blogs and MySpace.

Courtesy www.GuidedImageryDownloads.com

Figure 5-6: A product offering for The Healing Waterfall guided meditation begins on Facebook and links to the corresponding page on the primary website to continue the process.

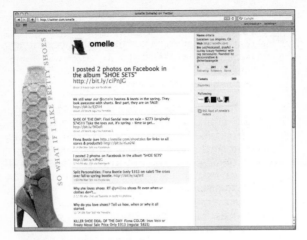

Courtesy Angelle & LaFave, LLC dba Omelle

Figure 5-7: Omelle, a luxury footwear site, links visitors from its Twitter feed to its online store.

By comparison, a *virtual storefront* either imports products from an existing online store or allows products to be uploaded directly to a freestanding, online store. At the add-to-cart stage, these storefronts link to your regular Webstore or to a third-party site to process the transactions. Though virtual storefront strategies may be a useful way to cast a wider net for customers, they may complicate your recordkeeping when used in addition to an existing Webstore.

E-commerce tools, which let you promote and sell only your own products, are quite different from social shopping services, which aggregate products from multiple sources — often suggested by consumers themselves — and link viewers back to your website.

Freestanding e-commerce tools that link to PayPal or other third-party services generally don't integrate with inventory and accounting packages as might a full-featured, on-site shopping cart. If you don't link to your existing cart, you may need to adjust those records manually.

If you use a virtual storefront in addition to an existing on-site store, but don't track inventory automatically, there's another way to track the source of sales. You could create separate SKUs for products that will be listed on different online store locations or at a different price for tracking purposes; for example, items specifically discounted for your audience on Twitter. This approach wouldn't work with automated inventory controls. Some virtual storefront options are listed in the following sections.

Cartfly

Cartfly operates in a manner similar to Netcarnation (see the next section) but doesn't take data from an existing store. You create an independent online store that you can then replicate elsewhere, as long as the site accepts HTML. You can install your store display on MySpace, Friendster, Hi5, Perfspot, Blogger, Xanga, TypePad, Tagworld, Facebook (which has a separate installation procedure), and other sites.

Cartfly (`cartfly.com`) is unique in offering to let your friends and followers "share" your store, almost as though the store were a YouTube video. By copying and pasting your "share" code on their own websites, social media pages, or blogs, your friends can generate dozens of online points of sale. It's like having push carts all over town.

Free to set up and use, Cartfly charges a 3 percent transaction fee on all sales. It defaults to Amazon for payment processing, so you need to set up an Amazon merchant account as well; PayPal is available as an alternative. This option is reasonable if you have no existing online store but want to start selling on the web.

Netcarnation

Netcarnation Marketplace (netcarnation.com), a virtual storefront tool, supports customizable displays on Facebook, MySpace, Hi5, Orkut, Ning, and Friendster. A mini-storefront can appear on your profile page as well. It imports product information from many platforms, including Zen Cart, Etsy, Amazon, and eBay.

If you have no existing Webstore, you can upload individual products and integrate Netcarnation with a PayPal shopping cart.

Netcarnation comes in free or premium versions. The free version, which is ad-supported, displays as many as ten products. It's perfect if you're just dipping a toe into e-commerce or if you want to feature a subset of your products for a particular audience. The premium version, for $1 per month, accepts as many as 1,000 products and includes multiple-site displays, integration, and promotion.

Premium Netcarnation storefronts can be managed from any of the sites on which they appear. For instance, when you add, delete, or edit products on Facebook, the changes automatically appear on your other selected sites, such as MySpace or Ning.

ProductCart

The ProductCart "ECommerce Widget for Blogs" is designed for its own customers to use. It's an easy way for ProductCart (www.earlyimpact.com) store owners to redisplay products taken from their website store on a blog, a social networking page, or another site. Free with the purchase of the shopping cart, the widget is generated in one click from the user Control Panel.

Operation is straightforward. First, the Webstore manager designates specific items in the store catalog as "portable." The widget dynamically loads the selected product information from the store database and displays it on the page where the widget is placed. Simply copy and paste the generated code into any blogging platform or another site that supports JavaScript. For some sites, such as Facebook and MySpace, you must place the widget by using Widgetbox.

When viewers click on items in the ProductCart widget, they link to the existing ProductCart store on your site. The advantages of this approach lie in already centralized inventory and reporting functions.

The ProductCart widget is also an easy way to help affiliates, if you have them. Because they can attach their IDs to the product links, they can also easily use the widget on their own blogs or websites, reducing the amount of support you may need to provide. By treating different social media sites as affiliates, you can identify sales generated by each source.

 You might want to offer a special sale price or discount just for members of a particular social network. If your shopping cart doesn't provide a linkable widget — but supports promotion codes — you can always advertise a promotion code, in text or as a graphic, on your social profile pages.

Sellit

Sellit (www.sellit.com) works like Netcarnation, importing products from Yahoo!, CafePress, Etsy, or

Cartfly stores and reproducing product offerings in a Flash-based widget on a blog or elsewhere. Developed by the same team as Cartfly, it works in a similar manner but accepts material from elsewhere. You simply register and paste in your existing shop URL. Sellit does the rest.

Like Cartfly, Sellit offers a Shout icon so that you can post your store on multiple sites and others can distribute it, as long as the destination site accepts an embedded web application. The Shout function is compatible with Twitter, Facebook, social bookmarking sites, and most blogs.

Basic services are free, with a $12 per month solution for Sellit Pro, which accepts up to 150 products and offers advanced features and additional advertising impressions.

Shopit

Shopit (www.shopit.com) takes a distinctly different approach. Billing itself as "empowering every Internet user to be a merchant," Shopit is an ad-supported social network itself, but it contains a built-in store for selling products or services.

You can quickly upload items for sale and build a custom widget that's distributed to other social networks, blogs, and e-mails. The widget drives visitors from those sites (for example, from MySpace, Facebook, LinkedIn, Plaxo, Bebo, Friendster, eBay, Craigslist, or blogs) back to a Shopit-hosted storefront.

Though listings are free, Shopit charges a transaction fee and runs through PayPal.

Keeping Your Ear to the Social Ground

The onslaught of data from social media sites can be overwhelming. To garner some value from all the noise, you can take advantage of certain tools to monitor what's being said about your company.

 Social media monitoring is about who's saying what. It's about your brand, your products, and your reputation. It's not the same as *social media measurement,* which deals with traffic statistics, conversion rates, and return on investment.

 Bring user feedback directly to you. Place a free feedback widget on your site from `http://feedback.widget.me`, `http://crowdsound.com`, or `www.makeuseof.com/dir/snapabug-visual-feedback`. More elaborate versions are available for a fee from GetSatisfaction.com. This feature takes some programming knowledge; if you're not up to the task, ask your programmer.

You can find some monitoring tools for specific types of services in the sections that follow.

Deciding what to monitor and why

If you didn't have anything else to do, you could monitor everything. That situation isn't realistic, so you need to set some constraints. Start with your goal and ask yourself what you want to accomplish. For example, you may want to

✔ Track what's being said, both positive and negative, about your company and products.

✔ Conduct competitor or market research.

✔ Stay up-to-date on what's happening in
   your industry.

✔ Watch trends over time in terms of mentions,
   topics of interest, or volume of comments.

✔ Gain a competitive advantage.

✔ Monitor the success of a specific press release,
   media campaign, or product promotion.

✔ Monitor for infringement of trademark or other
   intellectual property.

✔ Obtain customer feedback so you can improve
   your products and services.

After you've decided your goal, it should be obvious
what search terms or keywords to monitor. Your list
might include the following:

✔ Your company name

✔ Your domain name

✔ Names of executives and staff who speak with
   the public

✔ Product names and URLs

✔ Competitors' names

✔ Keywords

✔ Topic tags

Deciding which tools to use

The number of monitoring tools is almost as great as the
amount of data they sift through. Research your options
and choose at least one tool that monitors across

multiple types of social media. Depending on the social media services you're using, you might want to select one from each appropriate service category as well.

The frequency with which you check results from these tools will depend on the overall visibility of your company, the schedule for your submissions to different services, and the overall intensity of your social media presence. For some companies, it might be a daily task. For others, once a week or even once a month will be enough.

If you're not sure where to start, begin with weekly Google Alerts to monitor the web and daily Social Mention alerts to monitor social media. Add one tool each for blogs and Twitter, if you use them actively or think people may be talking about your business on their own. Adjust as needed.

Using free or cheap social monitoring tools

Pick one or more of the tools in this section to monitor across multiple types of social media.

Mark your choices on your Social Media Marketing Plan. If the tool doesn't offer automated reporting, you'll need to enter the submission task, as well as the review task, on your Social Media Activity Calendar.

Addictomatic: Inhale the Web

Addictomatic (http://addictomatic.com/about) lets you "instantly create a custom page with the current buzz on any topic." It searches hundreds of live sites including news, blog posts, videos, and images, and offers a personalized dashboard that you can bookmark and return to for updates.

Alterian SM2

Alterian (http://alterianSM2.com), formerly
Techrigy, monitors and measures social media, stores
the results, and allows in-depth analyses. The free
version allows you to store up to five profiles and
1,000 search results per query. You can customize
reports and view multiple characteristics of social
mentions, as shown in Figure 5-8.

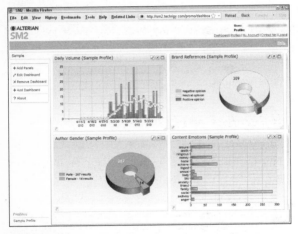

Figure 5-8: The Alterian dashboard displays information about
social mentions in graphic format.

BrandsEye

BrandsEye (www.brandseye.com) claims to compre-
hensively track every online mention of your brand to
protect your reputation. The basic package for $1/
month offers twice-daily updates on five phrases.

Google Alerts

One of the easiest and most popular of the free monitoring services, Google Alerts (www.google.com/alerts) are notifications of new results on up to 1,000 search terms. Alerts can be delivered via e-mail, your iGoogle page, or RSS feed.

You can receive results for news articles, websites, blogs, video, Google groups, or a comprehensive version, which comprises news, web, and blog results.

You set the frequency with which Google checks for results and other features on a Manage Your Alerts page. Think of Alerts as an online version of a "clipping" service. Yahoo! (http://alerts.yahoo.com) offers something similar.

Google Trends

Google Trends (www.google.com/trends) compares how frequently searches have been made on up to five topics over time, how frequently those terms have appeared in Google News, and the geographic location that generated the searches.

HowSociable?

Type any brand name at www.howsociable.com to see how visible it is in social media. It's great for monitoring competitors.

monitorThis

A free aggregator for up to 26 search engine feeds covering websites, blogs, microblogs, articles, news, photos, video, and tags, monitorThis (http://monitorthis.info) is a manual search on a single term. Results can be sorted by publication date or search engine.

Moreover Technologies

Moreover (http://w.moreover.com/public/free-rss/free-feeds.html) offers free RSS feeds from thousands of news and social media sources, enabling you to track your company, your competitors, and a nearly endless list of keywords and topics. For in-depth business intelligence, their Social Media Metabase (http://w.moreover.com/public/products/social-media-metabase.html) searches and monitors hundreds of thousands of blogs, podcasts, video-sharing sites, photo-sharing sites, microblogs, wikis, reviews, and forums on a paid basis.

PostRank Analytics

PostRank (https://analytics.postrank.com) monitors something it calls "engagement" on a variety of social media services. It quantifies how often individuals take action after reviewing a particular piece of content (for example, a blog post), which it calls an engagement event. For instance, tweeting, posting a comment, or voting one digg would constitute an event. PostRank integrates with Google Analytics. It costs $9 per month or $99 per year to track five sites, with a 30-day free trial.

Social Mention

Social Mention (http://socialmention.com) tracks and measures what is being said about a specific topic in real time across more than 100 social media services. It provides a social ranking score based on "popularity" for every search. Figure 5-9 shows the results for the term "Twitter."

You can select to monitor only specific services and choose among service categories of bookmarks, blogs, microblogs, comments, news, networks, video,

audio, images, Q&A, or all. While you can input only
one term at a time, if you set up social alerts (http://
socialmention.com/alerts), you can receive
daily reports — much like Google Alerts — for
multiple terms compiled into a spreadsheet.

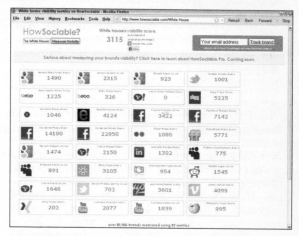

Courtesy of Social Mention

Figure 5-9: Social Mention provides a social ranking score based
on its definition of strength, sentiment, passion, and reach.

In addition, Social Mention aggregates trends (www.
socialmention.com/trends), in near real time,
about social media discourse. This feature is handy
for market research.

Social Mention also offers real-time widgets
(http://socialmention.com/tools) to
place on your site or in your browser bar. The
browser is a simple plug-in, but your programmer will need to copy and paste the widget code
onto your site.

Trackur

Trackur (www.trackur.com) tracks all forms of social media including blogs, news, networks, RSS feeds, Tweets, images, and video. In addition to displaying conversational content, it presents trends over time and analyzes any website mentioning a term being monitored. You can get a free account with one saved search and unlimited results. Monthly plans with updates twice/hour start at $18/month.

WhosTalkin.com

WhosTalkin.com (www.whostalkin.com) is another free, real-time search tool. It surveys 60 social media services for current conversations in the categories of blogs, news, networks, videos, images, forums, and tags. It lacks the reporting capabilities of Social Mention, but it does include actual comments. WhosTalkin.com provides results for only one term at a time, but offers a browser search plug-in and an iGoogle gadget.